CLASSIC
SALADS

CLASSIC
SALADS

OVER 70 SENSATIONAL RECIPES FOR CLASSIC AND CONTEMPORARY SALADS

CONSULTANT EDITOR
CHRISTINE INGRAM

LORENZ BOOKS
LONDON • NEW YORK • SYDNEY • BATH

First published in the UK in 1997 by Lorenz Books

© 1997 Anness Publishing Limited

Lorenz Books is an imprint of
Anness Publishing Limited
Hermes House
88–89 Blackfriars Road
London SE1 8HA

This edition is distributed in Canada by Book Express, an imprint of
Raincoast Books Distribution Limited

ISBN 1 85967 360 0

A CIP catalogue record for this book is available from the British Library

Publisher: Joanna Lorenz
Senior Cookery Editor: Linda Fraser
Project Editor: Anne Hildyard
Designer: Siân Keogh
Photography: Karl Adamson, David Armstrong, Edward Allwright,
Steve Baxter, James Duncan, Amanda Heywood and Patrick McLeavey
Food for Photography: Jacqueline Clark, Kit Chan, Jane Hartshorn,
Jane Stevenson, Steven Wheeler and Carole Handslip
Illustrator: Madeleine David
Stylists: Blake Minton, Kirsty Rawlings and Hilary Guy

Printed in Singapore by Star Standard Industries Pte. Ltd.

1 3 5 7 9 10 8 6 4 2

NOTES
For all recipes, quantities are given in both metric and imperial measures and,
where appropriate, measures are also given in standard cups and spoons. Follow
one set, but not a mixture because they are not interchangeable.

Standard spoon and cup measurements are level.
1 tsp = 5ml, 1 tbsp = 15ml, 1 cup = 250ml/8fl oz

Australian standard tablespoons are 20ml. Australian readers should use 3 tsp in
place of 1 tbsp for measuring small quantities of gelatine, cornflour, salt etc.

Size 3 (medium) eggs should be used unless otherwise stated.

CONTENTS

INTRODUCTION

Salads must be one of the most satisfying dishes to prepare. Visually, as well as in texture and flavour, they are ideal – colourful, fresh and varied. There's no limit to the fabulous salads an imaginative cook can create.

It is almost impossible to say what defines a salad. They are frequently made with raw ingredients, but cooked pulses, grains or other vegetables are equally in order. They are often served cold, but many are warm – perhaps served with a hot dressing or with grilled meat or fish. Their role in a meal is no clue either: salads make a perfect accompaniment, but almost every cuisine in the world has its favourite main course salad too – from Gado-Gado in Indonesia to Italy's excellent pasta salads. Perhaps a salad's most defining feature is the dressing. Classically this is made using oil and vinegar, although all sorts of other ingredients can be used. However, the purpose is always the same – to unite all the separate elements of the salad into a glorious whole.

There are no rules on what can or cannot go into a salad, although green salad leaves are among the favourites. Vegetables and fruit, whether raw or cooked, should however be absolutely fresh, while cooked ingredients like rice or pasta should be cooked *al dente*, so that they retain some bite to give the salad texture.

SALAD GREENS

Cos lettuce – has a firm texture and slightly nutty flavour.

Little Gem – has a firm heart and a distinct, pleasant flavour.

Curly endive (frisée) and *escarole* – are members of the chicory family. They have a distinct, slightly bitter flavour that is best combined with sweeter leaves like lamb's lettuce or iceberg.

Radicchio – is a member of the chicory family and has a similar bitter flavour. It is a favourite salad leaf, not only for its flavour but for its beautiful colouring – deep wine-red leaves with cream ribs.

Batavian endive – is similar to escarole but has a slightly sweeter taste. It can withstand a well-flavoured dressing.

Iceberg lettuce – although fairly mild in flavour, this lettuce has a wonderful crunchy texture and is good mixed with more strongly flavoured leaves, like frisée or watercress.

Lollo rosso – is a loose-leafed lettuce with a mild flavour. Valued for its superb purple-red colour, this lettuce is best mixed with stronger flavoured salad leaves.

Lollo biondo – is similar in flavour to lollo rosso, and has a pretty curly edge.

Oak leaf lettuce – is a loose-leafed lettuce with a mild pleasant flavour. The leaves range from pale green, through pink to a deep maroon.

Lamb's lettuce (corn salad) – is a delicious, slightly sweet flavoured leaf that makes a wonderful addition to a salad, or can be used as a garnish by itself.

Rocket (arugula) – is a deservedly popular leaf with a distinct pepper-lemon flavour. Add to milder flavoured leaves, like iceberg or oak leaf lettuce.

Spinach – the young leaves make a wonderful salad, either mixed with other leaves or by themselves. They have an excellent rich flavour and are extremely nutritious, being a good source of vitamins A, B and C and of iron, when eaten raw. Remove stalks if rough.

Watercress – is strong tasting with a peppery flavour. Excellent when combined with milder flavoured leaves.

OTHER SALAD VEGETABLES

While salad leaves often form the basis of a salad, almost all vegetables can be used, either as part of the salad, or as the main ingredient. Many recipes have vegetables simply prepared and served raw, but sometimes they can be steamed or grilled to add an interesting and delicious dimension to a dish.

Celery – use white or green celery, remove the strings and slice finely.

Fennel – use raw, cut into fine julienne strips, or blanch first and add to mixed salads. It has a distinct and sharp aniseed flavour and tastes best with blander vegetables, and with a creamy dressing.

Cucumber – with its clean, crisp texture, cucumber is excellent in many salad dishes with a well-flavoured dressing.

Clockwise from top left: Batavian endive, lollo rosso, lollo biondo, escarole, oak leaf lettuce, lamb's lettuce, spinach, watercress, rocket, frisée, cos, iceberg and Little Gem.

Cabbage – very finely sliced white cabbage mixed with grated carrot makes the ever popular coleslaw. Chinese cabbage, either served raw or briefly steamed or stir-fried, is popular in many Chinese or Thai salad dishes.
Carrots – with their wonderful sweet flavour, carrots are invaluable in salads. They can be grated and mixed with a caraway seed dressing, or cut into julienne strips for a variety of salads.
Courgettes – unless very young, when they only need to be thinly sliced, courgettes are best when briefly steamed with herbs. They too can have a starring role in a salad, and go well with a yogurt or soured cream dressing.
Onions and *spring onions* – mild flavoured onions, like red or Spanish onions, cut into thin rings are excellent in tomato salads, dressed with a good olive oil. Spring onions are great in mixed salads, or added to a green salad.
Green beans – trim and then cook these for a few minutes, either steaming or boiling in the minimum of water until just tender. Drain and refresh under cold running water. Green beans make a superb salad by themselves, served with chopped tomatoes, onions and garlic, or they can be added to other green salads.
Asparagus – steam until tender and add to green salads for a real luxury flavour.
Mushrooms – provide texture to a salad. Fresh button mushrooms can be sliced and used in mixed salads, or featured more strongly with peanuts or cashew nuts and avocado or banana for an unusual but delicious side salad. Wipe clean with damp kitchen paper.
Tomatoes – an essential salad ingredient, added to mixed salads or better still given a starring role in salads like Salata Tricolore – tomatoes, mozzarella and fresh basil. Buy top quality tomatoes for salads, preferably those on the vine, which have the best flavour.
Avocado – with a soft texture and mild flavour, avocados make a wonderful addition to mixed green salads. Sprinkle the flesh with lemon juice after slicing to prevent it discolouring.

A selection of vegetables for using in salads includes potatoes, celery, fennel, tomatoes, turnips, garlic, spring onions, mushrooms, courgettes, baby corn, carrots and French beans.

Peppers – these are another versatile salad vegetable. Slice them and add raw to bean salads or roast or grill them and serve with garlic, tomatoes and olive oil for a rich Italian salad. To peel peppers, char them under a hot grill until the skin blackens and then place in a plastic bag. Close tightly and then when cool enough to handle, peel off the outer skin.

FRUIT

Fruit, of course, comes into its own in fruit salads, but there is a place for fruit in many savoury salads as well – tomatoes, avocados and peppers are fruits, don't forget. When using fruit in salads, use it to complement other flavours. Apples, with their crisp texture and pleasant sweet taste, are nice when combined with softer ingredients, such as avocado. Pears are excellent in all sorts of salads – try them with rocket or other strongly flavoured leaves. Citrus fruits, such as oranges and grapefruit, add astringency to a salad. They also go well in pasta salads with fennel or celery, with a creamy dressing to bring the flavours together. Fruit is particularly useful in elegant, large salads where each separate ingredient is prepared and laid out by itself. As well as adding colour, their sweeter flavour contrasts with the more bitter salad ingredients. Pineapple, for instance, is essential in Gado-Gado, but also consider melon and grapes for antipasto.

Using Herbs

Herbs are as essential in salads as other vegetables. Not only do they add their distinctive flavour, but when added to dressings or mayonnaise, they subtly change the character of a salad, so that you can enhance a particular flavour or stress a certain characteristic, simply by adding basil, or mint, for instance.

Many herbs can be added in whole sprigs to mixed green salads. Like this, they contrast with the flavour of other leaves, providing a delicious variety of tastes. Alternatively, herbs can be finely chopped and added to dressings, where they add a more diffuse flavour to the whole salad. Mint, for instance, sharpens a salad and is good with Turkish and Middle Eastern dishes.

Herbs are invariably better when fresh, and nowadays it is easy to buy fresh herbs all year round. If you can grow your own, so much the better, but little window-sill pots are the next best thing, meaning you have a good fresh supply for several weeks at a time.

Basil – with its pungent warm flavour, this is a favourite in many salads and essential for any Italian insalata. The leaves can be used whole and mixed into leafy salads, sprinkled over tomato salads with olive oil, or chopped and used in dressings.

Mint – unmistakable and clean tasting, mint adds freshness without masking other flavours. Use it in dressings, or finely chop it and add to salads.

Thyme – another of the warm, earthy herbs, with a characteristic blunt lemon flavour. Part of its appeal is its heady aroma, which can be detected if used in dressings. Use thyme by itself or with parsley, garlic and marjoram.

Parsley – there are two main types of parsley: curly and flat leaf. Both have a fresh, faintly lemony flavour, more apparent in flat leaf parsley. Finely chopped, and used with marjoram, it adds a pleasant herby taste to dressings. Used in sprigs in salads, its characteristic flavour is more noticeable, and can enhance a plain green salad.

Clockwise from top left: thyme, flat leaf parsley, chives, lavender, rose petals, mint and basil.

Chives – unlike onions, to whose family they belong, chives have the virtue of having that characteristic flavour without taking over the whole dish. Chives exemplify what's best about herbs – they add subtle reminders of other tastes, without cloaking flavours. Chives can be snipped over salads, or added to dressings and mayonnaise.

Marjoram – sweet and fragrant, the fresh leaves can be sprinkled on to salads, or added to dressings.

Tarragon – with its faintly aniseed and vanilla flavour, tarragon is best used in salads with fish or eggs, or used to flavour mayonnaise.

Coriander – this fragrant herb is delicious added to mixed green salad, adding a distinct pungency against the bitter frisée or sweet lamb's lettuce. Shop bought coriander from Indian foodstores can be very pungent indeed, but home grown or locally grown coriander is much milder. Not so good in spicy dishes, but still wonderful in salads.

Garlic

Garlic adds a unique flavour – it is perhaps the most important of all dressing ingredients. If very finely chopped, it can be sprinkled over tomato salads. However, garlic is mostly used in dressings, such as vinaigrette, mayonnaise, yogurt and herb. Don't use garlic indiscriminately, as it will take over given half a chance. However, for Provençal, Mediterranean or Greek salads, garlic is essential. To use in a dressing, crush a small bulb with the back of a knife, or use a garlic crusher if liked.

Spices

While herbs add a subtle, fresh flavour to food, spices are more assertive, adding either pungency or heat and if used in moderation bringing out the flavour of other ingredients. Spices should be used carefully, especially in salads, where flavours are delicate and can be overwhelmed by headier tastes.

Used carefully, however, you'll be surprised how a dash of ground coriander or a hint of cayenne pepper can enhance a salad or perk up a dressing, and for many Asian salads, a pinch of spice is essential.

Pepper – either black or white, this is the most popular spice in the West. It enhances the flavour of food by exciting the taste buds. The majority of Western savoury dishes use a little pepper. Black pepper is milder than white. Always grind your own pepper, as ready-ground pepper has a bland taste.

Celery salt – is a combination of celery seed and salt, and is useful in salads as it brings out the flavour of vegetables.

Cayenne pepper – is made from the dried, ground seeds and pods of the cayenne chilli pepper. It is slightly less fiery than chilli powder and can be used to spice up certain dressings.

Soy sauce – is made from fermented soya beans; light soy sauce is milder and less salty than the dark soy sauce. It is useful for adding body to dressings to go with pork, beef or duck salads.

Coriander – the seeds of coriander have a sweet orangey flavour, and ground coriander can be used in dressings for a fuller, more pungent flavour.

Other spices can be used sparingly for salads: cumin, cinnamon, cardamom and turmeric are all useful. If possible, always buy spices in small quantities, so that they do not sit around in the cupboard for months – or even years.

DRESSINGS

A dressing can make or break a salad. Well-made dressings should be a perfect blend of individual ingredients that harmonize with the leaves and vegetables, grains and meat or fish in the salad. Once you have spent time buying, preparing and arranging your salad, take extra time to make a well-flavoured and balanced dressing.

OILS

Most dressings are made using oils. The dressing binds the salad together and oil is the principal element, adding richness in flavour and texture. Strongly flavoured oils add a wonderful fragrance to a dressing, but their flavour needs to be tempered with milder oils.

Olive oil – this is the king of all oils,

with a rich fragrance and flavour. The best olive oil is extra virgin olive oil, where hand-picked olives are cold-pressed to give an almost perfect flavour. The olives for virgin olive oil are picked mechanically and often warmed before pressing for higher extraction of oil. Other standard olive oils are suitable for frying, but for salads buy virgin or better still extra virgin olive oil. For some dressings and for some palates, sunflower or safflower oil can be blended with olive oil for a milder but still satisfying flavour.

Seed and nut oils – sunflower and groundnut oil are mild, neutral oils, valued as such as they are useful as a base for stronger flavoured oils. You can use half sunflower, half olive oil for dressings, and mayonnaise can be made entirely with sunflower oil, so that other flavours can be appreciated. Walnut and hazelnut oil have a distinct nutty flavour and make excellent dressings for certain salads. A little will go a long way, and sunflower oil can be blended with nut oils with excellent results.

Garlic oil – make your own flavoured oil by steeping 2–3 crushed garlic cloves in sunflower or, if preferred, olive oil for 1–2 hours. This will add a subtle garlic flavour to dressings, and can also be used for frying croûtons or other ingredients.

OTHER DRESSING INGREDIENTS

Vinegars – unless a recipe calls for something particular, a simple white wine vinegar is all you need for most dressings and mayonnaise.

Lemon and lime juice – add astringency. Take care not to use too freely, as they have a similar strength to vinegar.

Mustard – useful to add a depth of flavour and to act as an emulsifier. Dijon mustard, unless *fort*, is mild and suitable for most dressings, but English mustard is good when serving a salad with sausages or grilled meats.

MAKING SALADS

If making a mixed or leaf salad, choose leaves that give contrast in texture and colour as well as flavour. Add fresh herbs for further contrasts in flavours.

MAKING DRESSINGS

Make a dressing in the proportion of five parts of oil, to one of vinegar or lemon juice. Season with salt and pepper and add French mustard and garlic according to the recipe or to preference. If liked, a pinch of sugar can also be added, which blunts the flavour. Dressings can be made using a whisk, in a blender or shaken in a jar.

From left: Italian olive oil, Spanish olive oil, Italian olive oil, safflower oil, hazelnut oil, walnut oil, groundnut oil, French olive oil, Italian olive oil, wine vinegar and garlic oil.

SALAD STARTERS

*Salads are a perfect way to start a meal. Leafy salads combined
with a cocktail of seafood, cheese or spicy meats are deliciously tasty,
but are still light enough to complement the main course. Smoked
Trout Salad or Egg and Tomato Salad with Crab are both favourite
starters: simple to prepare, yet with an elegance to
grace any dinner party. For a more substantial starter, or possibly
a light lunch, try Summer Tuna Salad or Spinach Salad
with Bacon and Prawns.
Alternatively, mix and match various salads for
an interesting buffet spread.*

Egg and Tomato Salad with Crab

Chilli sauce and horseradish give this dressing a pleasant piquancy.

INGREDIENTS

Serves 4
lettuce leaves
2 x 200g/7oz cans crabmeat, drained
4 hard-boiled eggs, sliced
16 cherry tomatoes, halved
½ green pepper, seeded and thinly
    sliced
6 black olives, stoned and sliced

For the dressing
250ml/8fl oz/1 cup mayonnaise
10ml/2 tsp fresh lemon juice
45ml/3 tbsp chilli sauce
½ green pepper, seeded and finely
    chopped
5ml/1 tsp prepared horseradish
5ml/1 tsp Worcestershire sauce

1 To make the dressing, place all the ingredients in a bowl and mix well. Set aside in a cool place.

2 Line four plates with lettuce leaves. Mound the crabmeat in the centre. Arrange the eggs around the outside with the tomatoes on top.

3 Spoon some of the dressing over the crabmeat. Arrange the green pepper slices on top and sprinkle with the olives. Serve immediately with the remaining dressing.

Summer Tuna Salad

This colourful salad is perfect for a summer lunch in the garden – use canned or freshly cooked salmon in place of the tuna, if you like.

INGREDIENTS

Serves 4–6
175g/6oz radishes
1 cucumber
3 celery sticks
1 yellow pepper
175g/6oz cherry tomatoes, halved
4 spring onions, thinly sliced
45ml/3 tbsp lemon juice
45ml/3 tbsp olive oil
2 x 200g/7oz cans tuna, drained
    and flaked
30ml/2 tbsp chopped fresh parsley
salt and black pepper
lettuce leaves, to serve
thin strips twisted lemon rind,
    to garnish

1 Cut the radishes, cucumber, celery and yellow pepper into small cubes. Place in a large, shallow dish with the cherry tomatoes and spring onions.

2 In a small mixing bowl, stir together the salt and lemon juice with a fork until dissolved. Pour this over the vegetable mixture. Add the oil and black pepper to taste. Stir to coat the vegetables. Cover and set aside for 1 hour.

3 Add the drained and flaked tuna and chopped parsley to the mixing bowl and toss gently until everything is well combined.

4 Arrange the lettuce leaves on a serving platter and spoon the salad into the centre. Garnish with the strips of lemon rind.

Avocado and Papaya Salad

INGREDIENTS

Serves 4

2 ripe avocados
1 ripe papaya
1 large orange
25−50g/1−2oz small rocket leaves or
  lamb's lettuce
1 small red onion, thinly sliced

For the dressing

60ml/4 tbsp olive oil
30ml/2 tbsp lemon or lime juice
salt and black pepper

1 Halve the avocados and remove the stones. Carefully peel off the skin, then cut each avocado half lengthwise into thick slices.

2 Peel and cut the papaya in half lengthwise. Scoop out the seeds and set aside 5ml/1 tsp for the dressing. Cut each papaya half into eight slices.

3 Peel the orange and cut out the segments, cutting either side of the dividing membranes.

4 Combine the dressing ingredients in a small bowl and mix well. Stir in the reserved papaya seeds.

5 Assemble the salad on four individual serving plates. Alternate slices of papaya and avocado. Add the orange segments and a small mound of rocket topped with onion rings. Spoon over the dressing.

Mango, Tomato and Red Onion Salad

This salad makes an appetizing starter; the under-ripe mango has a subtle sweetness and the flavour blends well with the tomato.

INGREDIENTS

Serves 4

1 firm under-ripe mango
2 large tomatoes or 1 beefsteak
  tomato, sliced
½ red onion, sliced into rings
½ cucumber, peeled and thinly sliced
30ml/2 tbsp sunflower or vegetable oil
15ml/1 tbsp lemon juice
1 garlic clove, crushed
2.5ml/½ tsp hot pepper sauce
sugar, to taste
salt and black pepper
snipped chives, to garnish

1 Cut away two thick slices either side of the mango stone and cut into slices. Peel the skin from the slices.

2 Arrange the mango, tomato, onion and cucumber slices on a large serving plate.

3 Blend the oil, lemon juice, garlic, hot pepper sauce, salt and black pepper in a blender or food processor, or place in a small jar and shake vigorously. Add a pinch of sugar to taste and mix again.

4 Pour the dressing over the salad and garnish with snipped chives.

Spinach Salad with Bacon and Prawns

Serve this hot salad with plenty of crusty bread for mopping up the delicious juices.

INGREDIENTS

Serves 4

105ml/7 tbsp olive oil
30ml/2 tbsp sherry vinegar
2 garlic cloves, finely chopped
5ml/1 tsp Dijon mustard
12 cooked king prawns
115g/4oz streaky bacon, rinded and cut into strips
about 115g/4oz fresh young spinach leaves
½ oak leaf lettuce, roughly torn
salt and black pepper

1 To make the dressing, whisk together 90ml/6 tbsp of the olive oil with the vinegar, garlic, mustard and seasoning in a small pan. Heat gently until thickened slightly, then keep warm.

2 Carefully peel the prawns, leaving the tails intact. Set aside.

3 Heat the remaining oil in a frying pan and fry the bacon until golden and crisp, stirring occasionally. Add the prawns and stir-fry for a few minutes until warmed through.

4 While the bacon and prawns are cooking, arrange the spinach and torn oak leaf lettuce leaves on four individual serving plates.

5 Spoon the bacon and prawns on to the leaves, then pour over the hot dressing. Serve at once.

Smoked Trout Salad

The pungent spiciness of horseradish makes it as good a partner with smoked trout as it is with roast beef. Either fresh or bottled horseradish can be used. In this recipe it combines with yogurt to make a delicious light salad dressing.

INGREDIENTS

Serves 4

1 oak leaf or other red lettuce
225g/8oz small tomatoes, cut into thin wedges
½ cucumber, peeled and thinly sliced
4 smoked trout fillets, about 200g/7oz each, skinned and flaked

For the dressing
pinch of English mustard powder
15–20ml/3–4 tsp white wine vinegar
30ml/2 tbsp light olive oil
100ml/3½fl oz/scant ¾ cup natural yogurt
about 30ml/2 tbsp grated fresh or bottled horseradish
pinch of caster sugar

COOK'S TIP

Salt should not be necessary in this recipe because of the saltiness of the trout.

1 First, make the dressing. Mix together the mustard powder and vinegar, then gradually whisk in the oil, yogurt, horseradish and sugar. Set aside for 30 minutes.

2 Place the lettuce leaves in a large bowl. Stir the dressing again, then pour half of it over the leaves and toss lightly using two spoons.

3 Arrange the lettuce on four individual plates with the tomatoes, cucumber and trout. Spoon over the remaining dressing and serve at once.

Mushroom Salad

This is a simple and refreshing salad. Letting it stand for a few hours before serving brings out the sweetness in the mushrooms.

INGREDIENTS

Serves 4

175g/6oz white mushrooms
grated rind and juice of ½ lemon
about 30−45ml/2−3 tbsp crème
  fraîche or soured cream
salt and white pepper
15ml/1 tbsp snipped fresh chives, to
  garnish

COOK'S TIP

If you prefer, toss the white mushrooms in a little dressing – made by whisking 60ml/4 tbsp walnut oil or extra virgin olive oil into the lemon juice.

1 Trim and slice the mushrooms thinly and place in a mixing bowl. Add the lemon rind and juice and the cream, adding a little more cream if needed. Stir gently to mix, then season with salt and white pepper. Leave the salad to stand for at least 1 hour.

2 Stir occasionally then serve, sprinkled with snipped chives.

Lamb's Lettuce and Beetroot Salad

This salad makes a colourful and unusual starter.

INGREDIENTS

Serves 4

150−175g/5−6oz lamb's lettuce,
  washed and roots trimmed
250g/9oz/3 or 4 small beetroot,
  cooked, peeled and diced
30ml/2 tbsp chopped fresh parsley

For the dressing

30−45ml/2−3 tbsp white wine vinegar
  or lemon juice
20ml/1 heaped tbsp Dijon mustard
2 garlic cloves, finely chopped
2.5ml/½ tsp sugar
120ml/4fl oz/½ cup sunflower or
  grapeseed oil
120ml/4fl oz/½ cup crème fraîche or
  double cream
salt and black pepper

1 First make the dressing. Mix the vinegar or lemon juice, mustard, garlic, sugar, salt and pepper in a small bowl, then slowly whisk in the oil until the sauce thickens.

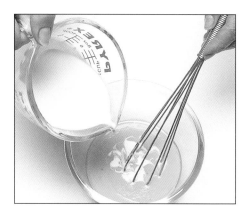

2 Lightly beat the crème fraîche or double cream to lighten it slightly, then whisk it into the dressing.

3 Toss the lettuce with a little of the vinaigrette and arrange on a serving plate or in a bowl.

4 Spoon the beetroot into the centre of the lettuce and drizzle over the remaining dressing. Sprinkle with chopped parsley and serve at once.

Raw Vegetables with Olive Oil Dip

This colourful antipasto from Rome is usually served with a dip made only from olive oil and salt.

INGREDIENTS

Serves 6–8
3 large carrots, peeled
2 fennel bulbs
6 celery sticks
1 pepper
2 large tomatoes or 12 cherry tomatoes
8 spring onions
12 radishes, trimmed
12 small cauliflower florets

For the dip
120ml/4fl oz/½ cup extra virgin olive oil
45ml/3 tbsp fresh lemon juice and
  4 fresh basil leaves, torn into small
  pieces (optional)
salt and black pepper

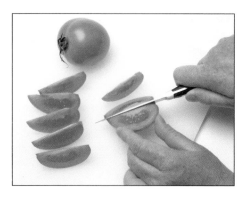

1 Prepare the vegetables by slicing the carrots, fennel, celery and pepper into small sticks.

2 If using large tomatoes, cut into sections, or leave cherry tomatoes whole. Trim the roots and dark green leaves from the spring onions. Arrange all the vegetables on a large platter, leaving space in the centre for the dip.

3 Make the dip by pouring the olive oil into a small bowl. Add salt and pepper and stir in the lemon juice and basil, if using. Place the bowl in the centre of the vegetable platter.

Celery Stuffed with Gorgonzola

If possible, prepare this dish just before serving.

INGREDIENTS

Serves 4–6
12 crisp celery sticks, leaves left on
75g/3oz/½ cup Gorgonzola cheese
75g/3oz/½ cup cream cheese
snipped fresh chives, to garnish

1 Wash and dry the celery sticks and trim the root ends.

2 In a small bowl, mash the cheeses together until smooth.

3 Fill the celery sticks with the cheese mixture, using a palette knife to smooth the filling. Chill for 30–45 minutes before serving. Garnish with snipped chives.

COOK'S TIP

Use another soft and creamy blue cheese in place of the Gorgonzola, if you prefer – or choose a strong flavoured Cheddar and grate it before adding to the cream cheese.

MAIN COURSE
SALADS

Give a salad centre stage in a meal and you're likely to find that it is not only star of the show, but one of the leading lights of your whole repertoire. Salads such as Seafood Salad with Fragrant Herbs or Tangy Chicken Salad are among the most perfectly balanced meals — meat, fish, cheese or pulses give the necessary protein, while the vegetables provide a wide range of essential vitamins and minerals. A satisfying salad should also contain beans, potatoes, rice or pasta, and even if you are planning a low-calorie meal, don't skimp on carbohydrates, but just leave out rich dressings. Use a low-fat dressing, or a dressing of finely chopped herbs, together with lemon and lime juice, which provides flavour without the calories.

Warm Salmon Salad

Guests will love this light refreshing salad. Serve it for lunch or for a healthy dish on a summer's evening.

INGREDIENTS

Serves 4

450g/1lb salmon fillet, skinned
30ml/2 tbsp sesame oil
grated rind of ½ orange
juice of 1 orange
5ml/1 tsp Dijon mustard
15ml/1 tbsp chopped fresh tarragon
45ml/3 tbsp groundnut oil
115g/4oz fine green beans, trimmed
175g/6oz mixed salad leaves, such as young spinach, radicchio, frisée and oak leaf lettuce
15ml/1 tbsp sesame seeds
salt and black pepper

1 Cut the salmon into bite-size pieces, then make the dressing. Mix together the sesame oil, orange rind and juice, mustard, chopped tarragon and seasoning in a bowl. Set aside.

2 Heat the groundnut oil in a frying pan. Add the salmon pieces and fry for 3–4 minutes, until lightly browned but still tender inside.

3 While the salmon is cooking, blanch the green beans in boiling salted water for about 5–6 minutes, until tender yet crisp.

4 Add the dressing to the fried salmon, toss together gently and cook for 30 seconds. Remove the pan from the heat.

5 Arrange the salad leaves on four serving plates. Drain the beans and toss them over the leaves. Spoon over the salmon with the cooking juices and serve immediately, sprinkled with the sesame seeds.

Prawn and Artichoke Salad

Artichokes and prawns are a popular combination in the southern states of America. This particular salad comes from Louisiana and the sharp, garlicky dressing is a typical Creole flavour.

INGREDIENTS

Serves 4

1 garlic clove
10ml/2 tsp Dijon mustard
60ml/4 tbsp red wine vinegar
150ml/¼ pint/ ¾ cup olive oil
45ml/3 tbsp shredded fresh basil leaves
    or 30ml/2 tbsp finely chopped
    fresh parsley
1 red onion, very finely sliced
350g/12oz cooked shelled prawns
400g/14oz can artichoke hearts
½ iceberg lettuce
salt and black pepper

1 Chop the garlic, then crush it to a pulp with 5ml/1 tsp salt, using the flat side of a heavy knife.

2 Blend the garlic and mustard to a paste, then add the vinegar and finally the olive oil, beating well to make a thick creamy dressing. Season with black pepper and, if necessary, a little more salt.

3 Add the basil or parsley and then stir in the sliced onion. Leave to stand for 30 minutes at room temperature, stir in the prawns and chill in the fridge for 1 hour or until ready to serve.

4 Drain the artichoke hearts and halve each one. Shred the iceberg lettuce finely.

5 Make a bed of lettuce on a serving platter or on four individual salad plates and arrange the artichoke hearts on top.

6 Just before serving, spoon the prawns and onion over the artichoke salad and then pour the marinade over the top.

Seafood Salad with Fragrant Herbs

INGREDIENTS

Serves 4–6

250ml/8fl oz/1 cup fish stock
    or water
350g/12oz squid, cleaned and cut
    into rings
12 uncooked king prawns, shelled
12 scallops
50g/2oz bean thread noodles, soaked
    in warm water for 30 minutes
juice of 1–2 limes
30ml/2 tbsp fish sauce
½ cucumber, cut into thin sticks
1 stalk lemon grass, finely chopped
2 kaffir lime leaves, finely shredded
2 shallots, finely sliced
30ml/2 tbsp chopped spring onion
30ml/2 tbsp chopped fresh coriander
12–15 mint leaves, roughly torn
3–4 red chillies, seeded and sliced
sprigs of fresh coriander, to garnish

1 Pour the stock or water into a medium-size saucepan, set over a high heat and bring to the boil.

2 Cook each type of seafood separately in the stock. Don't overcook – it takes only a few minutes for each seafood. Drain and set aside.

3 Drain the bean thread noodles and cut them into short lengths, about 5cm/2in long. Combine the noodles with the cooked seafood.

4 Blend the lime juice and fish sauce and mix with the cucumber, lemon grass, kaffir lime leaves, shallots, spring onion, herbs and chillies. Toss with the seafood noodles and spoon on to a large serving platter. Garnish with coriander and serve.

> ── COOK'S TIP ──
>
> Kaffir lime leaves, also known as citrus or lime leaves, have a unique flavour. They are available fresh or dried from most Asian delicatessens.

Pomelo Salad

A pomelo is a type of citrus fruit, with a sharp but sweet flesh.

INGREDIENTS

Serves 4–6
For the dressing
30ml/2 tbsp fish sauce
15ml/1 tbsp sugar
30ml/2 tbsp lime juice

For the salad
30ml/2 tbsp vegetable oil
4 shallots, finely sliced
2 garlic cloves, finely sliced
1 large pomelo or pink grapefruit
15ml/1 tbsp roasted peanuts
115g/4oz cooked shelled prawns
115g/4oz fresh cooked crabmeat
10–12 small mint leaves
2 spring onions, finely sliced
2 red chillies, seeded and finely sliced,
    fresh coriander leaves and shredded
    fresh coconut (optional), to garnish

1 Whisk together the fish sauce, sugar and lime juice and set aside.

2 Heat the oil in a small frying pan, add the shallots and garlic and fry until lightly brown. Transfer with a slotted spoon to a plate.

3 Peel the pomelo and break the flesh into small pieces, taking care to remove all the membranes.

4 Coarsely grind the peanuts into a large bowl, then add the pomelo, prawns, crabmeat, mint leaves and the fried shallot mixture. Add the dressing and toss well to mix. Arrange on a serving plate and sprinkle with the spring onions, red chillies, coriander leaves and shredded coconut, if using.

Prawn and Tuna Salad

INGREDIENTS

Serves 4

115g/4oz cooked peeled prawns
1 garlic clove, crushed
7.5ml/½ tbsp vegetable oil
2 eggs, hard-boiled
1 yellow plantain, halved
a few lettuce leaves
2 tomatoes
1 red pepper
1 avocado
juice of 1 lemon
1 carrot
200g/7oz can tuna or sardines
1 green chilli, seeded and
  finely chopped
30ml/2 tbsp chopped spring onion
salt and black pepper

1 Put the prawns in a small bowl, add the garlic and a little seasoning.

2 Heat the oil in a small saucepan, add the prawns and cook over a low heat for a few minutes. Transfer to a plate to cool.

3 Shell and cut the hard-boiled eggs into slices.

4 Boil the plantain in a pan of water for 15 minutes, cool, then peel and slice thickly.

5 Shred the lettuce and arrange on a large serving plate. Slice the tomatoes and red pepper and peel and slice the avocado, sprinkling it with a little lemon juice. Cut the carrot into matchstick-size pieces and arrange over the lettuce with the other vegetables.

6 Add the plantain, eggs, prawns and tuna fish or sardines. Sprinkle with the remaining lemon juice, scatter the chilli and spring onion on top and season with salt and pepper to taste. Serve as a lunch-time salad or as a delicious side dish.

— COOK'S TIP —

For a more substantial salad, use more prawns. Any types of lettuce can be used. Choose a variety of leaves for interesting colour and flavour.

Tangy Chicken Salad

Thai cuisine often features fresh salad leaves, together with water chestnuts, herbs and nuts combined with spicy poultry or fish. The chicken is marinated and cooked before being sliced, and the coconut and lime dressing brings the two elements together in perfect harmony.

INGREDIENTS

Serves 4–6
4 skinned, boneless chicken breasts
2 garlic cloves, crushed
30ml/2 tbsp soy sauce
30ml/2 tbsp vegetable oil
120ml/4fl oz/½ cup coconut cream
30ml/2 tbsp fish sauce
juice of 1 lime
30ml/2 tbsp sugar
115g/4oz water chestnuts, sliced
50g/2oz cashew nuts, roasted
4 shallots, finely sliced
4 kaffir lime leaves, finely sliced
1 stalk lemon grass, finely sliced
5ml/1 tsp finely chopped galangal or
    fresh root ginger
1 large red chilli, seeded and finely sliced
2 spring onions, finely sliced
10–12 mint leaves, torn
1 lettuce, shredded
sprigs of coriander, to garnish
2 red chillies, seeded and sliced, to garnish

2 Grill the chicken for 4–5 minutes on both sides, until cooked.

3 In a small saucepan, heat the coconut cream, fish sauce, lime juice and sugar. Stir until all of the sugar has dissolved and then remove from the heat.

5 Pour the coconut dressing over the chicken mixture and stir well. Spread lettuce over a large serving plate and spoon the chicken mixture on top. Garnish with sprigs of coriander and sliced red chillies.

1 Trim the chicken breasts of any excess fat and put them in a large dish. Sprinkle with the garlic, soy sauce and 15ml/1 tbsp of the oil. Leave to marinate for 1–2 hours.

4 Cut the cooked chicken into strips and mix with the water chestnuts, cashew nuts, shallots, kaffir lime leaves, lemon grass, galangal, red chilli, spring onions and mint leaves.

COOK'S TIP

Galangal is a member of the ginger family and looks very similar to ginger. If not available from Asian stores, use fresh root ginger instead.

Spicy Szechuan Noodle Salad

INGREDIENTS

Serves 4

350g/12oz thick noodles
175g/6oz cooked chicken, shredded
50g/2oz roasted cashew nuts

For the dressing
4 spring onions, chopped
30ml/2 tbsp chopped fresh coriander
2 garlic cloves, chopped
30ml/2 tbsp smooth peanut butter
30ml/2 tbsp sweet chilli sauce
15ml/1 tbsp soy sauce
15ml/1 tbsp sherry vinegar
15ml/1 tbsp sesame oil
30ml/2 tbsp olive oil
30ml/2 tbsp chicken stock or water
10 toasted Szechuan peppercorns,
    ground

1 Cook the noodles in a saucepan of boiling water until just tender, following the directions on the packet. Drain, rinse under cold running water and drain well.

2 While the noodles are cooking, combine all the ingredients for the dressing in a large bowl and whisk together well.

3 Add the noodles, shredded chicken and cashew nuts to the dressing, toss gently to coat and adjust the seasoning to taste. Serve at once.

VARIATION

You could substitute cooked turkey or pork for the chicken to make a change.

Sesame Noodle Salad with Spring Onions

This warm salad can be prepared and cooked in just a few minutes. If you can't find Chinese sesame paste, use tahini paste instead.

INGREDIENTS

Serves 4

2 garlic cloves, roughly chopped
30ml/2 tbsp Chinese sesame paste or
    tahini paste
15ml/1 tbsp dark sesame oil
30ml/2 tbsp soy sauce
30ml/2 tbsp rice wine
15ml/1 tbsp clear honey
pinch of five-spice powder
350g/12oz soba or buckwheat noodles
4 spring onions, finely sliced diagonally
50g/2oz beansprouts
7.5cm/3in piece of cucumber, cut
    into matchsticks
toasted sesame seeds
salt and black pepper

1 Process the garlic, sesame paste, oil, soy sauce, rice wine, honey and five-spice powder with a pinch each of salt and pepper in a blender or food processor until smooth.

2 Cook the noodles in a saucepan of boiling water until just tender, following the directions on the packet. Drain the noodles immediately and tip them into a bowl.

3 Toss the hot noodles with the dressing and the spring onions. Top with the beansprouts, cucumber and sesame seeds and serve.

COOK'S TIP

Soba are thin, brownish noodles made from buckwheat flour. They are available from Japanese delicatessens.

Pork and Rice Vermicelli Salad

INGREDIENTS

Serves 4

225g/8oz lean pork
2 garlic cloves, finely chopped
2 slices fresh root ginger, finely
   chopped
30−45ml/2−3 tbsp rice wine
45ml/3 tbsp vegetable oil
2 stalks lemon grass, finely chopped
10ml/2 tsp curry powder
175g/6oz beansprouts
225g/8oz rice vermicelli, soaked in
   warm water until soft and drained
½ lettuce, finely shredded
30ml/2 tbsp chopped fresh mint leaves
lemon juice and fish sauce, to taste
salt and ground black pepper
2 spring onions, finely sliced, 25g/1oz
   roasted peanuts, finely chopped, and
   pork crackles (optional), to garnish

1 Cut the pork in strips and put in a dish with half the garlic and ginger. Pour on 30ml/2 tbsp of the rice wine, season, stir and marinate for 1 hour.

2 Fry the remaining garlic and ginger for a few seconds. Stir in the pork and juices, lemon grass and curry. Fry until golden. Add rice wine if needed.

3 Place the beansprouts in a sieve. Blanch them by lowering the sieve into a saucepan of boiling water for 1 minute, then drain and refresh under cold running water. Drain again. Using the same water, cook the rice vermicelli for 3−5 minutes until tender, drain and rinse under cold running water. Drain well and tip into a bowl.

4 Add the beansprouts, lettuce and mint leaves and season with the lemon juice and fish sauce. Toss lightly.

5 Divide the noodle mixture among four serving plates, making a nest on each. Spoon the pork mixture on top. Garnish with spring onions, peanuts and pork crackles, if using.

Thai Chicken Salad

This is a superb main meal salad and once you have prepared the various ingredients, it is simple to cook and assemble. Most of the Thai ingredients are available from Asian stores, but if you can't get roasted ground rice, see the Cook's Tip to make your own.

INGREDIENTS

Serves 4–6
450g/1lb minced chicken
1 stalk lemon grass, finely chopped
3 kaffir lime leaves, finely chopped
4 red chillies, seeded and chopped
60ml/4 tbsp lime juice
30ml/2 tbsp fish sauce
15ml/1 tbsp roasted ground rice
2 spring onions, sliced
30ml/2 tbsp coriander leaves
mixed salad leaves, cucumber and tomato slices, to serve
sprigs of mint, to garnish

COOK'S TIP

Use sticky, or glutinous, rice to make roasted ground rice. Put it in a frying pan and dry-roast until golden, then grind to a powder in a mortar and pestle, food processor or blender. Keep in an airtight container in a cool, dry place and use as required.

1 Heat a large non-stick frying pan. Add the minced chicken and cook in a little water.

2 Stir constantly until cooked; this will take about 7–10 minutes.

3 Transfer the cooked chicken to a large bowl with all the remaining ingredients. Mix thoroughly.

4 Arrange the mixed salad leaves, cucumber and sliced tomato on a large serving platter. Spoon the flavoured chicken mixture over the top of the salad and garnish with some sprigs of fresh mint.

Warm Duck Salad

The rich gamey flavour of duck provides the basis for this delicious salad. Serve it in late summer or autumn and enjoy the warm aroma of orange and coriander.

Ingredients

Serves 4

1 small orange, cut into half slices
2 boneless duck breasts
150ml/¼ pint/ ¾ cup dry white wine
5ml/1 tsp ground coriander
2.5ml/½ tsp ground cumin
30ml/2 tbsp caster sugar
juice of ½ small lime or lemon
45ml/3 tbsp olive oil
75g/3oz white bread, crusts removed
    and cut into fingers
½ escarole lettuce
½ frisée lettuce
30ml/2 tbsp sunflower oil
4 sprigs fresh coriander
salt and cayenne pepper

1 Place the orange slices in a small saucepan, cover with water and bring to the boil. Simmer for about 5 minutes, then drain and set aside.

2 Cut the skin of the duck breasts diagonally and rub with salt. Place a heavy frying pan over a steady heat and cook the breasts for 20 minutes, turning once, until they are medium-rare. Transfer to a warm plate, cover and keep warm. Pour away any excess fat from the pan.

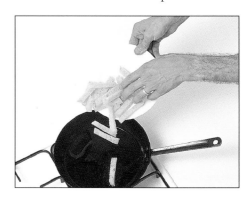

3 Heat the sediment in the pan until it begins to caramelize. Stir in the wine, then add the coriander, cumin, sugar and orange slices. Boil until fairly thick, then add the lime juice. Season with salt and cayenne pepper, then transfer to a bowl and keep warm.

4 Heat the olive oil in a frying pan and fry the bread until brown.

5 Toss the salad leaves in a little oil and arrange on four serving plates.

6 Slice the duck breasts diagonally and place on top of the salad. Spoon on the dressing, scatter with croûtons, decorate with a sprig of coriander and serve.

Salade Mouclade

This spectacular salad comes from La Rochelle in south-west France.

INGREDIENTS

Serves 4

60ml/4 tbsp olive oil
1 onion, finely chopped
350g/12oz/1¾ cups Puy or green
   lentils, soaked for 2 hours
900ml/1½ pints/3¾ cups vegetable
   stock
1.75kg/4–4½lb fresh mussels in
   their shells
75ml/5 tbsp white wine
2.5ml/½ tsp mild curry paste
1 pinch saffron
30ml/2 tbsp double cream
2 large carrots
4 celery sticks
900g/2lb young spinach, washed and
   stems removed
salt and cayenne pepper

1 Heat 45ml/3 tbsp of the olive oil in a heavy-based saucepan and fry the chopped onion for 6–8 minutes. Add the drained lentils and stock, bring to the boil and simmer for 45 minutes. Remove from the heat and cool.

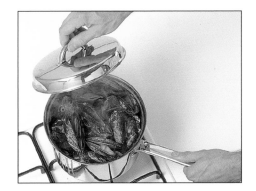

2 Clean the mussels thoroughly, discarding any that are damaged or do not close when sharply tapped. Place in a large saucepan, add the wine, cover and steam over a high heat for 12 minutes. Strain the mussels in a colander, collecting the cooking liquid in a bowl, and discarding any that have not opened. Cool, then take them out of their shells.

3 Strain the mussel liquid through a fine sieve into a small frying pan. Stir in the curry paste and saffron, then cook over a high heat until almost dry. Remove from the heat and stir in the double cream. Season and combine with the mussels.

4 Bring a saucepan of salted water to the boil. Cut the carrots and celery into 5cm/2in matchsticks, cook for 3 minutes, drain, cool and moisten with olive oil.

5 Place the spinach in a large pan, cover and steam for 2–3 minutes. Immerse in cold water and press the leaves dry with the back of a large spoon in a colander. Moisten with olive oil, season and set aside.

6 Spoon the lentils into the centre of four serving plates. Place five heaps of spinach around the edge of each one and arrange some carrot and celery on top. Spoon the mussels over the lentils and serve at room temperature.

Curly Endive Salad with Bacon

This country-style salad is popular all over France. When they are in season, dandelion leaves often replace the endive and the salad is sometimes sprinkled with chopped hard-boiled egg.

INGREDIENTS

Serves 4

225g/8oz curly endive or
    escarole leaves
75–90ml/5–6 tbsp extra virgin olive oil
175g/6oz piece of smoked bacon,
    diced, or 6 thick-cut smoked bacon
    rashers, cut crosswise into thin strips
50g/2oz white bread cubes
1 small garlic clove, finely chopped
15ml/1 tbsp red wine vinegar
10ml/2 tsp Dijon mustard
salt and black pepper

1 Tear the endive or escarole lettuce into bite-size pieces and put them in a salad bowl.

COOK'S TIP

Use endive or escarole leaves as soon as possible after purchase. To store, wrap the leaves and place in the salad drawer of the fridge for up to three days.

2 Heat 15ml/1 tbsp of the oil in a frying pan over a medium-low heat and add the bacon. Fry until browned, stirring occasionally. Remove with a slotted spoon and drain on kitchen paper.

3 Add 30ml/2 tbsp of oil to the pan and fry the bread cubes over a medium-high heat, turning frequently, until evenly browned. Remove with a slotted spoon and drain on kitchen paper. Wipe the pan clean.

4 Put the garlic, vinegar and mustard into the pan with the remaining oil and heat until just warm, whisking to combine. Season to taste, then pour over the salad and sprinkle with the fried bacon and croûtons.

Goat's Cheese Salad

INGREDIENTS

Serves 4

30ml/2 tbsp olive oil
4 slices of French bread, 1cm/½in
   thick
225g/8oz mixed salad leaves, torn in
   small pieces
2 firm goat's cheese rounds, about
   100g/4oz each, rind removed
1 yellow or red pepper, seeded and
   finely diced
1 small red onion, thinly sliced
45ml/3 tbsp chopped fresh parsley
30ml/2 tbsp snipped fresh chives

For the dressing

30ml/2 tbsp wine vinegar
5ml/1 tsp wholegrain mustard
75ml/5 tbsp olive oil

COOK'S TIP

For a substantial salad, use more salad leaves
and make double dressing. Add 115g/4oz
sliced cooked green beans to the leaves, and
toss with half the dressing. Top with the
cheeses and remaining dressing.

1 To make the dressing, mix the
vinegar and salt with a fork until
dissolved. Stir in the mustard.
Gradually stir in the oil until blended.
Season with pepper and set aside.
Preheat the grill.

2 Heat the oil in a frying pan. When
hot, add the bread and cook for
1 minute until golden. Turn and cook
the other side for 30 seconds more.
Drain on kitchen paper and set aside.

3 Place the salad leaves in a bowl.
Add 45ml/3 tbsp of the dressing
and toss to coat. Divide the dressed
leaves among four salad plates. Halve
each cheese, crossways.

4 Put the goat's cheeses, cut side up,
on a baking sheet and grill for
about 1–2 minutes until golden.

5 Set one goat's cheese on each slice
of bread and place in the centre of
each plate. Scatter the diced pepper,
red onion, parsley and chives over the
salad. Drizzle with the remaining
dressing and serve.

Warm Chicken Liver Salad

This popular salad makes an excellent light lunch or summer evening meal. For a rather more substantial dish, you could dry fry 3–4 rashers of chopped streaky bacon and toss them in with the salad at the end.

INGREDIENTS

Serves 4

115g/4oz each fresh young spinach
    leaves, rocket and lollo rosso lettuce
2 pink grapefruit
90ml/6 tbsp sunflower oil
10ml/2 tsp sesame oil
10ml/2 tsp soy sauce
225g/8oz chicken livers, chopped
salt and black pepper

1 Wash, dry and tear up all the spinach and salad leaves. Mix them together well in a large salad bowl.

2 Cut away the peel and white pith from the grapefruit, then segment them catching the juice in a bowl. Add the segments to the leaves in the bowl.

3 Mix 60ml/4 tbsp of the sunflower oil with the sesame oil, soy sauce, seasoning and grapefruit juice to taste.

4 Heat the rest of the sunflower oil in a small pan and cook the livers for 4–5 minutes, until firm and lightly browned, stirring occasionally.

5 Tip the chicken livers and dressing over the salad and serve at once.

COOK'S TIP

Chicken or turkey livers are often sold frozen. They are ideal for this recipe, and there's no need to leave them to defrost completely before cooking.

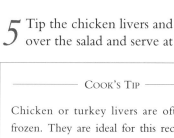

Pasta Salad with Broccoli and Artichokes

INGREDIENTS

Serves 4

105ml/7 tbsp olive oil

1 red pepper, quartered, seeded and
thinly sliced

1 onion, halved and thinly sliced

5ml/1 tsp dried thyme

45ml/3 tbsp sherry vinegar

450g/1lb pasta shapes, such as penne
or fusilli

2 x 175g/6oz jars marinated artichoke
hearts, drained and thinly sliced

150g/5oz cooked broccoli, chopped

20–25 black olives, stoned and
chopped

30ml/2 tbsp chopped fresh parsley

salt and black pepper

1 Heat 30ml/2 tbsp of the oil in a
non-stick frying pan. Add the red
pepper and onion and cook over a low
heat for 8–10 minutes, until just soft,
stirring occasionally.

2 Stir in the thyme, salt and vinegar.
Cook for 30 seconds more,
stirring, then set aside.

3 Bring a large pan of salted water to
the boil. Add the pasta and cook
until just tender (see packet instructions
for timing). Drain, rinse with hot
water, then drain again well. Transfer
to a large bowl. Add 30ml/2 tbsp of
the oil and toss well to coat.

4 Add the artichokes, broccoli,
olives, parsley, pepper and onion
mixture and remaining oil to the pasta.
Season with salt and pepper and stir to
mix. Leave to stand at least 1 hour
before serving, or chill overnight.

Spinach and Mushroom Salad

This is an excellent choice for anyone counting calories as it is very low in fat, yet still tasty with a variety of flavours and textures. Watercress or rocket would make a delicious addition.

INGREDIENTS

Serves 2–3
10 baby sweetcorn
115g/4oz mushrooms
2 tomatoes
1 small onion
20 small spinach leaves
25g/1oz salad cress
salt and black pepper
2 sprigs fresh coriander, to garnish
3–4 lime slices, to garnish

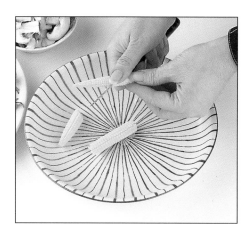

1 Halve the baby sweetcorn, and slice the mushrooms and tomatoes. Cut the onion into very thin rings.

2 Mix the spinach, baby sweetcorn, onion, mushrooms, tomatoes and salad cress together and arrange on a serving plate. Season with salt and pepper and garnish with fresh coriander and lime slices.

Nutty Bean and Pasta Salad

A vegetarian salad with a fiery hot dressing.

INGREDIENTS

Serves 4
1 onion, thinly sliced
115g/4oz/½ cup canned kidney beans, drained and rinsed
1 green courgette, sliced
1 yellow courgette, sliced
50g/2oz/1 cup pasta shells, cooked
50g/2oz/½ cup cashew nuts
25g/1oz/¼ cup peanuts
lime wedges, to garnish

For the dressing
120ml/4fl oz/½ cup fromage frais
30ml/2 tbsp natural low-fat yogurt
1 fresh green chilli, seeded and finely chopped
15ml/1 tbsp chopped fresh coriander
2.5ml/½ tsp salt
2.5ml/½ tsp black pepper
2.5ml/½ tsp crushed dried red chillies
15ml/1 tbsp lemon juice

1 Arrange the onion rings, kidney beans, courgette slices and pasta in a salad dish and sprinkle the cashew nuts and peanuts over the top.

2 Make the dressing in a separate bowl: blend the fromage frais, yogurt, green chilli, fresh coriander and salt and beat well using a fork.

3 Sprinkle the black pepper, crushed red chillies and lemon juice over the dressing. Garnish the salad with the lime wedges and serve with the dressing in a separate bowl or poured over the salad.

— VARIATION —

Instead of red kidney beans, add a mixture of beans such as chick-peas, cannellini beans and black-eyed beans. Add sliced cucumber rather than courgettes and vary the pasta shapes and nuts.

Mexican Mixed Salad

INGREDIENTS

Serves 4

45ml/3 tbsp white wine vinegar
5ml/1 tsp Dijon mustard
30ml/2 tbsp single cream
150ml/¼ pint/¾ cup vegetable oil, plus
    extra for frying
1 small garlic clove, finely chopped
5ml/1 tsp ground cumin
5ml/1 tsp dried oregano
450g/1lb lean minced beef
1 small onion, chopped
1.25ml/¼ tsp cayenne pepper
200g/7oz can sweetcorn, drained
425g/15oz can kidney beans, drained
15ml/1 tbsp chopped fresh coriander,
    plus extra coriander leaves, to garnish
1 small cos lettuce
3 tomatoes, sliced
225g/8oz/2 cups grated Cheddar cheese
1 avocado
50g/2oz/½ cup black olives, sliced
4 spring onions, thinly sliced
salt and black pepper
tortilla chips, to serve

1 To make the dressing, mix the vinegar and salt with a fork until dissolved. Stir in the mustard and cream. Gradually stir in the oil until blended, then add the garlic, cumin, oregano and pepper and set aside.

2 Heat 15ml/2 tsp vegetable oil in a large frying pan. Add the beef, onion, salt and cayenne and cook for 5–7 minutes, until just browned. Stir frequently to break up any lumps. Drain and leave to cool.

3 Toss the beef mixture, sweetcorn, kidney beans and coriander.

4 Stack the lettuce leaves on top of each other and shred them finely. Place in another bowl and toss with 45ml/3 tbsp of the dressing. Place the lettuce on four serving plates.

5 Mound the meat mixture in the centre. Arrange the tomatoes at the edges and sprinkle with the cheese.

6 Halve, stone, peel and dice the avocado and add to the plates. Scatter the olives and spring onions on top. Pour the remaining dressing over the salads and garnish with coriander. Serve with tortilla chips.

Thai Beef Salad

A hearty salad of beef, enlivened with a chilli and lime dressing.

INGREDIENTS

Serves 4

2 x 225g/8oz sirloin steaks
1 red onion, finely sliced
½ cucumber, finely sliced into
    matchsticks
1 stalk lemon grass, finely chopped
30ml/2 tbsp chopped spring onions
juice of 2 limes
15−30ml/1−2 tbsp fish sauce
2−4 red chillies, seeded and finely
    sliced, fresh coriander, Chinese
    mustard cress and mint leaves, to
    garnish

1 Pan-fry or grill the beef steaks to medium-rare. Allow to rest for 10−15 minutes.

2 When cool, use a sharp knife to slice the beef steaks thinly. Put the slices in a large bowl.

3 Add the sliced onion, cucumber matchsticks and lemon grass.

4 Add the spring onions. Toss and season with lime juice and fish sauce. Serve at room temperature or chilled, garnished with the chillies, coriander, mustard cress and mint.

CLASSIC SALADS

*Many countries have their favourite salads. Some are specialities of
particular regions, while others are "invented" by chefs for their clientele
and become associated with towns, villages, or just a restaurant or hotel.
As their popularity spreads further afield, these salads earn the title
"Classic Salads" and today there are many such examples. Indonesia's
Gado-Gado is a feast for the eyes and the palate and is deservedly world-
renowned. Salade Niçoise from Provence, with its delicious combination of
tuna, olives, beans and tomatoes, is another of the best known classic
salads. The Lebanese Tabbouleh mixes bulgur wheat with spring onions,
parsley and mint, and Caesar Salad, one of the most famous of salads,
has a rich dressing of egg, olive oil, lemon juice and anchovies.*

Salade Niçoise

INGREDIENTS

Serves 4

90ml/6 tbsp olive oil
30ml/2 tbsp tarragon vinegar
5ml/1 tsp tarragon or Dijon mustard
1 small garlic clove, crushed
115g/4oz French beans
12 small new or salad potatoes
3–4 Little Gem lettuces, roughly
   chopped
200g/7oz can tuna in oil, drained
6 anchovy fillets, halved lengthwise
12 black olives, stoned
4 tomatoes, chopped
4 spring onions, finely chopped
10ml/2 tsp capers
30ml/2 tbsp pine nuts
2 hard-boiled eggs, chopped
salt and black pepper
crusty bread, to serve

1 Mix the oil, vinegar, mustard, garlic and seasoning with a wooden spoon in a large salad bowl.

— COOK'S TIP —

Look for waxy salad potatoes such as Charlotte, Belle de Fontenay or Pink Fir.

2 Cook the French beans and potatoes in separate pans of boiling salted water until just tender. Drain and add to the bowl with the lettuce, tuna, anchovies, olives, tomatoes, spring onions and capers.

3 Just before serving, toast the pine nuts in a small frying pan until lightly browned.

4 Sprinkle over the salad while still hot, add the eggs and toss all the ingredients together well. Serve with chunks of hot crusty bread.

Caesar Salad

For this famous salad, created by the Tijuanan chef called Caesar Cardini in the 1920s, the dressing is traditionally tossed into crunchy cos lettuce, but any crisp lettuce will do.

INGREDIENTS

Serves 4
1 large cos lettuce
4 thick slices white or Granary bread
  without crusts, cubed
45ml/3 tbsp olive oil
1 garlic clove, crushed
25g/1oz/5 tbsp grated Parmesan cheese

For the dressing
1 egg
1 garlic clove, chopped
30ml/2 tbsp lemon juice
dash of Worcestershire sauce
3 anchovy fillets, chopped
120ml/4fl oz/½ cup olive oil
salt and black pepper

1 Preheat the oven to 220°C/425°F/ Gas 7. Separate, rinse and dry the lettuce leaves. Tear the outer leaves roughly and chop the heart. Arrange the lettuce in a large salad bowl.

2 Mix together the cubed bread, olive oil and garlic in a separate bowl until the bread has soaked up the flavoured oil. Lay the bread cubes on a baking sheet and place in the oven for about 6–8 minutes (keeping an eye on them) until golden brown. Remove and leave to cool.

3 To make the dressing, break the egg into the bowl of a food processor or blender and add the garlic, lemon juice, Worcestershire sauce and one of the anchovy fillets. Blend until smooth.

4 With the motor running, pour in the olive oil in a thin stream until the dressing has the consistency of single cream. Season with black pepper and a little salt if needed.

5 Pour the dressing over the salad leaves and toss well, then toss in the garlic croûtons, Parmesan cheese and the remaining anchovies and serve.

Tabbouleh

This classic Lebanese salad has become very popular in other countries. It makes an ideal substitute for a rich dish on a buffet table and is excellent served with cold sliced lamb.

INGREDIENTS

Serves 4
175g/6oz/1 cup fine bulgur wheat
juice of 1 lemon
45ml/3 tbsp olive oil
40g/1½oz fresh parsley, finely chopped
45ml/3 tbsp chopped fresh mint
4–5 spring onions, chopped
1 green pepper, seeded and sliced
salt and black pepper
2 large tomatoes, diced, and a few black olives, stoned, to garnish

1 Put the bulgur wheat in a bowl. Add enough cold water to cover the wheat and let it stand for at least 30 minutes and up to 2 hours.

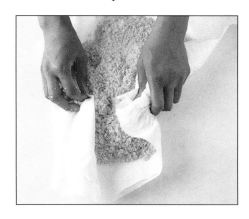

2 Drain and squeeze with your hands to remove excess water. The bulgur wheat will swell to double its original size. Spread on kitchen paper to allow it to dry completely.

3 Place the bulgur wheat in a large bowl, add the lemon juice, oil and a little salt and pepper. Leave to stand for 1–2 hours if possible, to allow the flavours to develop.

4 Add the chopped parsley, mint, spring onions and pepper and mix well. Garnish with diced tomatoes and olives and serve.

Yogurt with Cucumber

INGREDIENTS

Serves 4–6
½ cucumber
1 small onion
2 garlic cloves
1–2 sprigs fresh parsley
475ml/16fl oz/2 cups natural yogurt
1.5ml/¼ tsp paprika
salt and white pepper
mint leaves, to garnish
pitta bread (optional), to serve

1 Finely chop the cucumber and onion, crush the garlic and finely chop the parsley.

COOK'S TIP

It's not traditional, but other fresh herbs, such as mint or chives, would be equally good in this dish. Use a mild onion, or substitute 2 shallots.

2 Lightly beat the yogurt and then add the cucumber, onion, garlic and parsley and season with salt and pepper to taste.

3 Sprinkle with a little paprika and chill for at least 1 hour. Garnish with mint leaves and serve with warm pitta bread or as an accompaniment to meat, poultry and rice dishes.

New Potato and Chive Salad

The secret of a good potato salad is to mix the potatoes with the dressing while they are still warm, so that they absorb the flavour.

INGREDIENTS

Serves 4–6
675g/1½lb new potatoes (unpeeled)
4 spring onions
45ml/3 tbsp olive oil
15ml/1 tbsp white wine vinegar
3.75ml/ ¾ tsp Dijon mustard
175ml/6fl oz/ ¾ cup mayonnaise
45ml/3 tbsp snipped fresh chives
salt and black pepper

1 Cook the potatoes in boiling salted water until tender. Meanwhile, finely chop the white parts of the spring onions along with a little of the green part.

2 Whisk together the oil, vinegar and mustard. Drain the potatoes well, then immediately toss lightly with the oil and vinegar mixture and spring onions and leave to cool.

3 Stir the mayonnaise and chives into the potatoes with salt and pepper to taste. Chill well until ready to serve with grilled sausages, chicken wings or cold meats.

COOK'S TIP

Look out for the small, waxy potatoes, sold especially for salads and cold dishes – they are particularly good in this recipe.

Gado-Gado

Gado-Gado is a rightly famous salad from Indonesia. It always features a good variety of both cooked and raw ingredients and is consequently a colourful dish.

INGREDIENTS

Serves 6

2 unripe pears
1–2 eating apples
juice of ½ lemon
banana leaf or lettuce leaves
1 small crisp lettuce, shredded
½ cucumber, seeded, sliced and salted, set aside for 15 minutes, then rinsed and drained
6 small tomatoes, cut in wedges
3 slices fresh pineapple, cored and cut in wedges
3 eggs or 12 quail's eggs, hard-boiled and shelled
175g/6oz egg noodles, cooked, cooled and chopped
deep-fried onions

For the peanut sauce

2–4 fresh red chillies, seeded and ground, or 15ml/1 tbsp chilli sambal
300ml/½ pint/1¼ cups coconut milk
350g/12oz crunchy peanut butter
15ml/1 tbsp dark soy sauce or dark brown sugar
5ml/1 tsp tamarind pulp, soaked in 45ml/3 tbsp warm water, strained and juice reserved
coarsely crushed peanuts
salt

1 To make the peanut sauce, put the chillies or chilli sambal and coconut milk in a pan. Add the peanut butter and heat gently, stirring, until no lumps of peanut butter remain.

2 Allow to simmer gently until the sauce thickens, then add the soy sauce or sugar and tamarind juice. Season with salt to taste. Pour into a bowl and sprinkle with a few coarsely crushed peanuts.

3 Cut the unripe pears into matchsticks and slice the eating apples finely. Sprinkle all the fruit with lemon juice. Place the banana leaf or lettuce leaves on a flat platter and arrange the vegetables and fruit attractively on the top.

4 Slice or quarter the hard-boiled eggs (leave quail's eggs whole) and add to the salad with the chopped noodles and deep-fried onions.

5 Serve at once, accompanied by a bowl of the peanut sauce.

Melon and Crab Salad

INGREDIENTS

Serves 6

450g/1lb fresh crabmeat
120ml/4fl oz/½ cup mayonnaise
45ml/3 tbsp soured cream or
  natural yogurt
30ml/2 tbsp olive oil
30ml/2 tbsp lemon or lime juice
2–3 spring onions, finely chopped
30ml/2 tbsp finely chopped fresh
  coriander
1.25ml/¼ tsp cayenne pepper
1½ cantaloupe or small honeydew
  melons
3 chicory heads
salt and black pepper
fresh coriander sprigs, to garnish

1 Pick over the crabmeat very carefully, removing any bits of shell or cartilage. Leave the pieces of crabmeat as large as possible.

2 In a medium-size mixing bowl, combine all the other ingredients except the melons and the chicory heads and season to taste. Mix everything together well, then fold in the crabmeat and mix carefully.

3 Halve the cantaloupe or honeydew melons and remove and discard all the seeds. Cut the melons into thin slices, then remove the rind.

4 Arrange the salad on six individual serving plates, making a decorative design with the melon slices and the whole chicory leaves. Place a mound of dressed crabmeat on to each serving plate and garnish the salads with fresh sprigs of coriander.

Lettuce and Herb Salad

This classic salad is a good accompaniment for many dishes. It would be perfect served with most fish recipes, and it makes a refreshing side dish when served with roast meat.

INGREDIENTS

Serves 4
½ cucumber
mixed lettuce leaves
1 bunch watercress, about 115g/4oz
1 chicory head, sliced
45ml/3 tbsp mixed chopped fresh
  herbs such as parsley, thyme,
  tarragon, chives and chervil

For the dressing
15ml/1 tbsp white wine vinegar
5ml/1 tsp mustard
75ml/5 tbsp olive oil
salt and black pepper

COOK'S TIP

Never dress a salad until just before serving, as the lettuce leaves will wilt and become unpleasantly soggy if allowed to sit in dressing for too long.

1 To make the dressing, mix the vinegar and mustard together, then whisk in the oil and seasoning.

2 Peel the cucumber, if liked, then halve the cucumber lengthwise and scoop out the seeds. Thinly slice the flesh. Tear the lettuce leaves into bite-size pieces.

3 Either toss the cucumber, lettuce, watercress, chicory and herbs together in a bowl, or arrange them in the bowl in layers.

4 Stir the dressing, then pour it all over the salad, tossing it lightly to coat the salad vegetables and leaves. Serve at once.

Turkish Feta Salad

This popular salad makes an excellent light lunch. The saltiness of the cheese is balanced by the refreshing salad vegetables.

INGREDIENTS

Serves 4

1 cos lettuce heart
1 green pepper
1 red pepper
½ cucumber
4 tomatoes
1 red onion
225g/8oz/2 cups feta cheese, crumbled
black olives, stoned, to garnish

For the dressing

45ml/3 tbsp olive oil
45ml/3 tbsp lemon juice
1 garlic clove, crushed
15ml/1 tbsp chopped fresh parsley
15ml/1 tbsp chopped fresh mint
salt and black pepper

1 Chop the lettuce into bite-size pieces. Seed the peppers, remove the cores and cut the flesh into thin strips. Chop the cucumber and slice or chop the tomatoes. Cut the onion in half, then slice finely.

2 Place the chopped lettuce, peppers, cucumber, tomatoes and onion in a large bowl. Scatter the feta over the top and toss together lightly.

3 To make the dressing for the salad, blend together the olive oil, lemon juice and crushed garlic in a small bowl. Stir in the chopped fresh parsley and mint and season with a little salt and pepper, to taste.

4 Carefully pour the fresh dressing over the salad in the bowl, toss lightly and serve garnished with a handful of black olives.

Persian Cucumber Salad

This simple salad can be served with pretty well any dish – you can make it ahead of time, but don't add the dressing until just before you are ready to serve or the lettuce leaves will wilt.

INGREDIENTS

Serves 4

4 tomatoes
½ cucumber
1 onion
1 cos lettuce heart

For the dressing

30ml/2 tbsp olive oil
juice of 1 lemon
1 garlic clove, crushed
salt and black pepper

 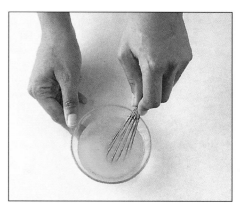

1 Cut the tomatoes and cucumber into small cubes. Finely chop the onion and tear the lettuce into pieces.

2 Place the tomatoes, cucumber, onion and lettuce in a large salad bowl and mix lightly together.

3 To make the dressing, pour the olive oil into a small bowl. Add the lemon juice, garlic and salt and blend together well. Pour over the salad and toss lightly to mix. Sprinkle with black pepper and serve with meat or rice dishes.

SIDE SALADS

In France, side salads are often served separately from the main course, partly to refresh the palate, and partly, no doubt, so that the diner can appreciate the individual tastes and textures of the salad. Elsewhere, salads are served alongside the main course, either sitting side by side in their own dish or served to the whole table in salad bowls. Whichever you prefer, a side salad makes a very good accompaniment to any main course. Leafy salads, like Citrus Green Leaf Salad with Croûtons, are excellent with almost any dish, but are particularly popular with pizzas and pasta dishes. Other side salads can feature a range of colourful vegetables – Roasted Pepper Salad looks and tastes wonderful and is lovely as part of a buffet, or with fish or poultry.

Cabbage Slaw with Date and Apple

Three types of cabbage are shredded together for serving raw, so that the maximum amount of vitamin C is retained, making this a crunchy as well as a nutritious salad.

INGREDIENTS

Serves 6–8
¼ small white cabbage, shredded
¼ small red cabbage, shredded
¼ small Savoy cabbage, shredded
175g/6oz/1 cup dried stoned dates
3 eating apples
juice of 1 lemon
10ml/2 tsp caraway seeds

For the dressing
60ml/4 tbsp olive oil
15ml/1 tbsp cider vinegar
5ml/1 tsp clear honey
salt and black pepper

1 Finely shred all the cabbages and place them in a large salad bowl.

2 Chop the dates and add them to the cabbage.

3 Core the eating apples, and slice them thinly into a mixing bowl. Add the lemon juice and toss together to prevent discoloration before adding to the salad bowl.

4 To make the dressing, combine the oil, vinegar and honey in a screw-top jar. Add salt and pepper, close the jar tightly and shake well. Pour the dressing over the salad, toss lightly, then sprinkle with the caraway seeds and toss again.

VARIATION

The dried dates in this dish give the salad a faintly Middle Eastern flavour. You could emphasize this flavour by substituting 25–40g/1–1½oz pine nuts for the caraway seeds. Dry fry them briefly until golden and then sprinkle over the salad before serving.

Sprouted Seed Salad

Beansprouts have a high vitamin content, a delicious crunchy texture and a delicate flavour.

INGREDIENTS

Serves 4
2 eating apples
115g/4oz alfalfa sprouts
115g/4oz beansprouts
115g/4oz aduki beansprouts
¼ cucumber, sliced
1 bunch watercress, trimmed
1 carton mustard and cress, trimmed

For the dressing
150ml/¼ pint/ ¾ cup low-fat natural yogurt
juice of ½ lemon
bunch of chives, snipped
30ml/2 tbsp chopped fresh herbs
ground black pepper

1 Core and slice the apples and mix with the other salad ingredients.

2 Mix the dressing ingredients in a jug. Drizzle over the salad and toss together just before serving.

COOK'S TIP

You can sprout the beans at home to ensure that they are really fresh. Always buy the beans from a health food shop and ask for those that are selected for sprouting.

Aubergine Salad

This interesting and unusual salad comes from Thailand.

INGREDIENTS

Serves 4–6

2 aubergines
15ml/1 tbsp vegetable oil
30ml/2 tbsp dried shrimps, soaked and drained
15ml/1 tbsp coarsely chopped garlic
1 hard-boiled egg, shelled and chopped
4 shallots, finely sliced into rings
fresh coriander leaves and 2 red chillies, seeded and sliced, to garnish

For the dressing

30ml/2 tbsp lime juice
5ml/1 tsp sugar
30ml/2 tbsp fish sauce

1 Grill or roast the aubergines until charred and tender.

2 When cool enough to handle, peel away the skin and slice the flesh.

VARIATION

For an interesting variation, try using salted duck's or quail's eggs, cut in half, instead of chopped hen's eggs.

3 Heat the oil in a small frying pan, add the drained shrimps and garlic and fry until golden. Remove from the pan and set aside.

4 To make the dressing, put the lime juice, sugar and fish sauce in a small bowl and whisk together until well blended.

5 To serve, arrange the sliced aubergines on a serving dish. Sprinkle with the chopped egg, shallots and dried shrimp mixture. Drizzle over the dressing and garnish with coriander and red chillies.

Peppery Bean Salad

INGREDIENTS

Serves 4–6

425g/15oz can kidney beans
425g/15oz can black-eyed beans
425g/15oz can chick-peas
¼ red pepper
¼ green pepper
6 radishes
15ml/1 tbsp chopped spring onion
5ml/1 tsp ground cumin
15ml/1 tbsp tomato ketchup
30ml/2 tbsp olive oil
15ml/1 tbsp white wine vinegar
1 garlic clove, crushed
hot pepper sauce, to taste
salt
sliced spring onion, to garnish

1 Drain the canned beans and chick-peas and rinse under cold running water. Shake off the excess water and tip them into a large salad bowl.

2 Core, seed and chop the peppers. Trim the radishes and slice thinly. Add to the beans with the peppers and spring onion.

3 Mix together the cumin, ketchup, oil, vinegar and garlic in a small bowl. Add a little salt and hot pepper sauce to taste and stir again thoroughly.

4 Pour the dressing over the salad and mix. Chill for at least 1 hour before serving, garnished with sliced spring onion.

COOK'S TIP

For an even tastier salad, allow the ingredients to marinate for a few hours.

Yogurt Salad

A delicious salad with a yogurt base, this is really an Eastern version of coleslaw. For a low-calorie dish, use low-fat yogurt.

INGREDIENTS

Serves 3–4
350ml/12fl oz/1½ cups natural yogurt
10ml/2 tsp clear honey
2 carrots, thickly sliced
2 spring onions, roughly chopped
115g/4oz cabbage, finely shredded
50g/2oz/¾ cup sultanas
50g/2oz/½ cup cashew nuts
16 white grapes, halved
2.5ml/½ tsp salt
5ml/1 tsp chopped fresh mint
3–4 mint sprigs (optional), to garnish

1 Using a fork, beat the yogurt in a bowl with the clear honey.

2 Mix together the carrots, spring onions, cabbage, sultanas, cashew nuts, grapes, salt and chopped mint.

----- COOK'S TIP -----

Serve this salad with kebabs or other barbecued meat or fish. It is also delicious as part of a buffet meal, served with other Middle Eastern appetizers, like dolmades, fried aubergines or falafels.

3 Pour the yogurt mixture over the salad ingredients and lightly toss together to mix.

4 Either chill the salad in the fridge for several hours or until required, or transfer to a large serving dish and serve at once. Garnish the salad with fresh mint sprigs, if wished.

Spicy Baby Vegetable Salad

This warm salad makes an excellent accompaniment to a variety of main course dishes.

INGREDIENTS

Serves 6
10 small new potatoes, halved
15 baby carrots
10 baby courgettes
115g/4oz/1½ cups button mushrooms

For the dressing
45ml/3 tbsp lemon juice
22.5ml/1½ tbsp olive oil
15ml/1 tbsp chopped fresh coriander
2 small green chillies, seeded and finely chopped
5ml/1 tsp salt

1 Wash and boil the potatoes and carrots until tender. Trim the courgettes and steam until tender. Drain all the vegetables and place in a serving dish with the mushrooms.

2 In a separate bowl, mix together the lemon juice, olive oil, chopped coriander, green chillies and salt until well blended.

3 Pour the dressing over the vegetables and toss to mix. Serve with grilled meat or fish.

Pepper, Cucumber and Tomato Salad

This simple, refreshing peasant salad is a popular dish all over the Middle East.

INGREDIENTS

Serves 4
1 yellow or red pepper
1 large cucumber
4–5 tomatoes
1 bunch spring onions
30ml/2 tbsp finely chopped fresh
    parsley
30ml/2 tbsp finely chopped fresh mint
30ml/2 tbsp finely chopped fresh
    coriander
2 garlic cloves, crushed
75ml/5 tbsp olive oil
juice of 2 lemons
salt and black pepper
2 pitta breads, to serve

1 Slice the pepper, discarding the seeds and core, then roughly chop the cucumber and tomatoes. Place them in a large salad bowl.

2 Trim and slice the spring onions. Add to the cucumber, tomatoes and pepper with the finely chopped parsley, mint and coriander.

3 To make the dressing, blend the garlic with the olive oil and lemon juice in a jug, then season to taste with salt and black pepper. Pour the dressing over the salad and toss lightly to mix.

4 Toast the pitta bread in a toaster or under a hot grill until crisp and then serve it alongside the salad.

VARIATION

If you prefer, make this salad in the traditional way. After toasting the pitta bread until crisp, crush it in your hand and then sprinkle it over the salad before serving. Alternatively, cut the pitta bread in half and open up to make pockets. Spoon the salad into the pockets for a Middle Eastern sandwich!

COOK'S TIP

Although the recipe calls for only 30ml/ 2 tbsp of each of the herbs, if you have plenty to hand, then you can add as much as you like to this aromatic salad.

Watercress and Potato Salad

New potatoes are equally good hot or cold, and this colourful, nutritious salad is an ideal way of making the most of them.

INGREDIENTS

Serves 4

450g/1lb small new potatoes, unpeeled
1 bunch watercress, trimmed
200g/7oz/1½ cups cherry tomatoes, halved
30ml/2 tbsp pumpkin seeds
45ml/3 tbsp low-fat fromage frais
15ml/1 tbsp cider vinegar
5ml/1 tsp brown sugar
salt and paprika

1 Cook the potatoes in lightly salted, boiling water until just tender, then drain and leave to cool.

2 Toss together the potatoes, watercress, tomatoes and pumpkin seeds in a bowl.

3 Place the fromage frais, vinegar, sugar, salt and paprika in a screw-top jar and shake well to mix. Pour over the salad just before serving.

VARIATION

To make Spinach and Potato Salad, substitute about 225g/8oz fresh baby spinach leaves for the watercress.

COOK'S TIP

If you are preparing this salad in advance, mix the dressing in the jar and toss with the salad just before serving.

Beetroot, Chicory and Orange Salad

A refreshing salad that goes well with grilled meats or fish. Alternatively, arrange it prettily on individual plates and serve as a summer starter.

INGREDIENTS

Serves 4
2 cooked beetroot, diced
2 chicory heads, sliced
1 large orange
60ml/4 tbsp low-fat natural yogurt
10ml/2 tsp wholegrain mustard
salt and black pepper

> ——— COOK'S TIP ———
>
> If you prefer, use a selection of leaves instead of just chicory. Choose slightly bitter leaves such as curly endive or escarole, along with strongly flavoured leaves like rocket or spinach. Tear the leaves into pieces before mixing with the beetroot.

1 Mix together the diced, cooked beetroot and sliced chicory in a large serving bowl.

2 Finely grate the rind from the orange. With a sharp knife, remove all the peel and white pith. Cut out the segments, catching the juice in a bowl, and add the segments to the salad.

3 Add the orange rind, yogurt, mustard and seasoning to the orange juice, mix thoroughly, then spoon over the salad.

Roasted Pepper Salad

This colourful salad is very easy and can be made up to a day in advance, as the sharp-sweet dressing mingles with the mild pepper flavours.

INGREDIENTS

Serves 4
3 large red, green and yellow peppers, halved and seeded
115g/4oz feta cheese, diced or crumbled
15ml/1 tbsp sherry vinegar or red wine vinegar
15ml/1 tbsp clear honey
salt and black pepper

1 Arrange the pepper halves in a single layer, skin side up on a baking sheet. Place the peppers under a hot grill until the skin is blackened and beginning to blister.

2 Lift the peppers into a plastic bag and close the end. Leave until cool, then peel off and discard the skin.

3 Arrange the peppers on a platter and scatter over the cheese. Mix together the vinegar, honey and seasoning, then sprinkle over the salad. Chill until ready to serve.

Thai Cabbage Salad

INGREDIENTS

Serves 4–6

30ml/2 tbsp fish sauce
grated rind of 1 lime
30ml/2 tbsp lime juice
120ml/4fl oz/½ cup coconut milk
30ml/2 tbsp vegetable oil
2 large red chillies, seeded and cut into
   thin strips
6 garlic cloves, finely sliced
6 shallots, finely sliced
1 small cabbage, shredded
30ml/2 tbsp roughly chopped roasted
   peanuts, to serve

1 Make the dressing by combining together the fish sauce, lime rind and juice and the coconut milk. Set aside until needed.

2 Heat the oil and stir-fry the chillies, garlic and shallots, until the shallots are crisp. Transfer to a plate.

3 Blanch the cabbage in boiling salted water for about 2–3 minutes, drain and place in a large bowl.

4 Stir the dressing into the cabbage, mix well, then transfer into a serving dish. Sprinkle with the fried shallot mixture and the roasted peanuts.

--- COOK'S TIP ---

Other vegetables, such as broccoli, cauliflower and beansprouts, can also be prepared in this way.

Green Bean Salad

You could make this lovely dish at any time of the year using imported or frozen vegetables and still get a pretty, healthy – and unusual – salad.

INGREDIENTS

Serves 4

175g/6oz shelled broad beans
115g/4oz French or flat beans,
    quartered
115g/4oz mange-touts
8–10 small fresh mint leaves
3 spring onions, chopped
60ml/4 tbsp green olive oil
15ml/1 tbsp cider vinegar
15ml/1 tbsp chopped fresh mint, or
    5ml/1 tsp dried
1 garlic clove, crushed
salt and black pepper

1 Plunge the broad beans into a saucepan of boiling water and bring back to the boil. Remove from the heat immediately and plunge into cold water. Drain. Repeat with the French or flat beans.

2 Mix together the blanched broad and French beans, the raw mange-touts, fresh mint leaves and chopped spring onions.

3 Blend the olive oil, vinegar, chopped mint, garlic and seasoning thoroughly, then pour over the salad and toss well. Chill until ready to serve.

Quick Ratatouille Salad

This salad is a delicious variation on the cooked dish. The key thing is that it keeps well – so well, in fact, it improves if eaten the next day.

INGREDIENTS

Serves 4
1 small aubergine, about 225g/8oz
60ml/4 tbsp olive oil
1 onion, sliced
1 green pepper, seeded and cut in strips
3 garlic cloves, crushed
15–30ml/1–2 tbsp cider vinegar
8 tiny firm tomatoes, halved
salt and mixed ground peppercorns
sprigs of oregano, to garnish

1 Slice and quarter the aubergine. Place in a colander and sprinkle with plenty of salt. Leave for 20 minutes and then drain off any liquid and rinse well under cold water.

2 Heat the oil in a large pan and gently sauté the onion, pepper and garlic, then stir in the aubergine and toss over a high heat for 5 minutes.

3 When the aubergine is beginning to turn golden, add the cider vinegar, tomatoes and seasoning to taste. Leave to cool, then chill well. Season to taste again before serving, garnished with sprigs of oregano.

--- COOK'S TIP ---

Once the aubergine is rinsed, squeeze dry in sheets of kitchen paper – the drier it is, the quicker it will cook and brown.

Crisp Fruity Salad

Crisp lettuce, tangy cheese and crunchy pieces of fruit make a refreshing salad for any occasion.

INGREDIENTS

Serves 4
½ Webb's lettuce
75g/3oz grapes, seeded and halved
50g/2oz/½ cup mature Cheddar cheese, grated
1 large eating apple, cored and thinly sliced
90–105ml/6–7 tbsp mild French vinaigrette (see Cook's Tip)
45ml/3 tbsp garlic croûtons

1 Tear the lettuce leaves into small pieces and place in a salad bowl. Add the grapes, cheese and apple.

2 Pour the dressing over the salad. Mix well and serve at once, sprinkled with garlic croûtons.

--- COOK'S TIP ---

Mix 15ml/1 tbsp French mustard, 15ml/1 tbsp white wine vinegar, pinch of sugar, seasoning with 60ml/4 tbsp sunflower oil.

Spicy Potato Salad

This tasty salad is quick to prepare, and makes a satisfying accompaniment to grilled or barbecued meat or fish.

INGREDIENTS

Serves 6
900g/2lb potatoes, peeled
2 red peppers
2 celery sticks
1 shallot
2–3 spring onions
1 green chilli
1 garlic clove, crushed
10ml/2 tsp finely snipped
   fresh chives
10ml/2 tsp finely chopped fresh basil
15ml/1 tbsp finely chopped fresh
   parsley
15ml/1 tbsp single cream
30ml/2 tbsp salad cream
15ml/1 tbsp mayonnaise
5ml/1 tsp mild mustard
7.5ml/½ tbsp sugar
snipped fresh chives, to garnish

1 Boil the potatoes in salted water until tender but still firm. Drain and cool, then cut into 2.5cm/1in cubes and place in a large salad bowl.

2 Halve the peppers, cut away and discard the core and seeds and cut into small pieces. Finely chop the celery, shallot and spring onions and slice the chilli very thinly, discarding the seeds. Add the vegetables to the potatoes together with the garlic and chopped herbs.

3 Blend the cream, salad cream, mayonnaise, mustard and sugar in a small bowl, stirring until the mixture is well combined.

4 Pour the creamy dressing over the prepared potato and vegetable salad and stir gently to coat it evenly. Serve the salad garnished with fresh snipped chives.

Sweet Potato and Carrot Salad

This salad has a sweet-and-sour taste, and can be served warm as part of a meal or eaten in a larger quantity as a main course.

INGREDIENTS

Serves 4

1 sweet potato
2 carrots, cut into thick diagonal slices
3 tomatoes
8–10 iceberg lettuce leaves
75g/3oz/½ cup canned chick-peas, drained

For the dressing
15ml/1 tbsp clear honey
90ml/6 tbsp low-fat natural yogurt
2.5ml/½ tsp salt
5ml/1 tsp black pepper

For the garnish
15ml/1 tbsp walnuts
15ml/1 tbsp sultanas
1 small onion, cut into rings

1 Peel the sweet potato and roughly dice. Boil until soft but not mushy, cover the pan and set aside.

2 Boil the carrots for just a few minutes, making sure they remain crunchy. Drain the water from the carrots and the sweet potato and place together in a bowl.

3 Slice the tops off the tomatoes, then scoop out and discard the seeds. Roughly chop the flesh.

4 Line a glass bowl with the lettuce leaves. Add the chick-peas and tomatoes to the sweet potato and carrots, mix well and then spoon into the salad bowl.

5 To make the dressing, blend together the clear honey, natural yogurt, salt and black pepper and beat well using a fork.

6 Garnish the salad with walnuts, sultanas and onion rings. Pour over the dressing, or serve it in a separate bowl, if wished.

COOK'S TIP

If liked, skin the tomatoes by plunging them into boiling water. (Don't seed them before doing this.) Leave for 1 minute, then remove and make a small slit in the skin with a knife. The entire skin should then slip off. Halve or quarter, remove seeds and then chop.

Mixed Green Salad

Mesclun is a ready-mixed Provençal green salad composed of several kinds of salad leaves and herbs. A typical combination might include rocket, radicchio, lamb's lettuce and curly endive with herbs such as chervil, basil, parsley and tarragon.

INGREDIENTS

Serves 4–6
1 garlic clove, peeled
30ml/2 tbsp red wine vinegar or sherry vinegar
5ml/1 tsp Dijon mustard (optional)
75–120ml/5–8 tbsp extra virgin olive oil
200–225g/7–8oz mesclun (mixed salad leaves and herbs)
salt and black pepper

1 Rub a large salad bowl with the garlic clove and leave in the bowl.

2 Add the vinegar, salt and pepper and mustard, if using. Stir to mix the ingredients and dissolve the salt, then whisk in the oil slowly.

3 Remove the garlic clove and stir the vinaigrette to combine. Add the salad leaves and herbs to the bowl and toss well. Serve at once.

VARIATION

Mesclun always contains some pungent leaves. When dandelion leaves are in season, they are usually found in the mixture, so use them when available.

Apple and Celeriac Salad

INGREDIENTS

Serves 3–4
1 large celeriac (about 675g/1½lb), peeled
10–15ml/2–3 tsp lemon juice
5ml/1 tsp walnut oil (optional)
1 eating apple
45ml/3 tbsp mayonnaise
10ml/2 tsp Dijon mustard
15ml/1 tbsp chopped fresh parsley
salt and black pepper

1 Shred the celeriac in a food processor or blender, or cut it into very thin julienne strips. Place it in a mixing bowl and sprinkle with the lemon juice and the walnut oil, if using. Stir well to mix.

2 Peel the apple, if you like, cut it into quarters and remove the core. Slice thinly crosswise and toss in with the celeriac.

3 Mix the mayonnaise, mustard and parsley, with salt and pepper to taste. Stir into the celeriac mixture. Chill for several hours before serving.

Bulgur Wheat Salad with Oranges and Almonds

INGREDIENTS

Serves 4

1 small green pepper
150g/5oz/1 cup bulgur wheat
600ml/1 pint/2½ cups water
¼ cucumber, diced
15g/½oz/½ cup chopped fresh mint
40g/1½oz/¾ cup flaked
  almonds, toasted
grated rind and juice of 1 lemon
2 seedless oranges
salt and black pepper
mint sprigs, to garnish

1 Using a sharp vegetable knife, carefully halve the green pepper. Discard the core and seeds, then cut the pepper into small cubes and set aside.

2 Place the bulgur wheat in a saucepan and add the water. Bring to the boil, lower the heat, cover and simmer for 10–15 minutes until tender. Alternatively, place the bulgur wheat in a heatproof bowl, pour over boiling water and leave to soak for 30 minutes. Most, if not all, of the water should be absorbed; drain off any excess.

3 Toss the bulgur wheat with the cucumber, green pepper, mint and toasted almonds in a serving bowl. Add the grated lemon rind and juice.

4 Cut the rind from the oranges, then working over the bowl to catch the juice, cut the oranges into neat segments. Add to the bulgur mixture, with seasoning, and toss lightly. Garnish with the mint sprigs.

Fruity Brown Rice Salad

An Asian-style dressing gives this colourful rice salad extra piquancy. Whole grains like brown rice are unrefined, so they retain their natural fibre, vitamins and minerals.

INGREDIENTS

Serves 4–6

115g/4oz/³/₄ cup brown rice
1 small red pepper, seeded and diced
200g/7oz can sweetcorn, drained
45ml/3 tbsp sultanas
225g/8oz can pineapple pieces in fruit juice
15ml/1 tbsp light soy sauce
15ml/1 tbsp sunflower oil
15ml/1 tbsp hazelnut oil
1 garlic clove, crushed
5ml/1 tsp finely chopped fresh root ginger
salt and black pepper
4 spring onions, sliced, to garnish

1 Cook the brown rice in a large saucepan of lightly salted boiling water for about 30 minutes, or until it is tender. Drain thoroughly and cool.

2 Tip the rice into a bowl and add the red pepper, sweetcorn and sultanas. Drain the pineapple pieces, reserving the juice, add them to the rice mixture and toss lightly.

3 Pour the reserved pineapple juice into a clean screw-top jar. Add the soy sauce, sunflower and hazelnut oils, garlic and root ginger. Add some salt and pepper. Then close the jar tightly and shake well to combine.

4 Pour the dressing over the salad and toss well. Scatter the spring onions over the top. The salad is delicious as part of a summer buffet or served with grilled meat or fish.

VARIATION

Try a mixture of brown rice and wild rice instead of just the brown rice. Cook the rice mixture for the recommended time.

Citrus Green Leaf Salad with Croûtons

Croûtons add a delicious crunch to leaf salads, while the kumquats or orange segments provide colour as well as a good helping of vitamin C.

INGREDIENTS

Serves 4–6
4 kumquats or 2 seedless oranges
200g/7oz mixed green salad leaves
4 slices of wholemeal bread, crusts removed
30–45ml/2–3 tbsp pine nuts, lightly toasted

For the dressing
grated rind of 1 lemon and 15ml/1 tbsp juice
45ml/3 tbsp olive oil
5ml/1 tsp wholegrain mustard
1 garlic clove, crushed

1 Thinly slice the kumquats, or peel and segment the oranges.

> — COOK'S TIP —
>
> Although not so low-calorie, croûtons are especially good fried. Make garlic oil by soaking 1 crushed garlic clove in 30–45ml/2–3 tbsp olive or sunflower oil for about 1 hour. Strain the oil into a pan and then fry the croûtons over a brisk heat until golden.

2 Tear all the salad leaves into bite-size pieces and place together in a large salad bowl.

3 Toast the bread on both sides and cut into cubes. Add to the salad leaves with the sliced kumquats or orange segments.

4 Shake all the dressing ingredients together in a jar. Pour over the salad just before serving and scatter the toasted pine nuts over the top.

Mixed Bean Salad with Tomato Dressing

All pulses are a good source of vegetable protein and minerals.

INGREDIENTS

Serves 4
115g/4oz French beans
425g/15oz can mixed pulses, drained and rinsed
2 celery sticks, finely chopped
1 small onion, finely chopped
3 tomatoes, chopped
45ml/3 tbsp chopped fresh parsley, to garnish

For the dressing
45ml/3 tbsp olive oil
10ml/2 tsp red wine vinegar
1 garlic clove, crushed
15ml/1 tbsp tomato chutney
salt and black pepper

1 Remove the ends from the French beans, then cook the beans in boiling water for 5–6 minutes (or steam for 10 minutes) until tender. Drain, then refresh under cold running water and cut into thirds.

2 Place the French beans and pulses in a large bowl. Add the celery, onion and tomatoes and toss lightly.

3 Shake the dressing ingredients together in a jar. Pour over the salad and sprinkle with the parsley.

> — COOK'S TIP —
>
> Cans of mixed beans are a good way of quickly adding colour and variety to a salad. They are normally made up of chick-peas, pinto, black-eyed, kidney, soya and aduki beans. Alternatively, you could choose a favourite bean for this salad. Pale green flageolets are very good. Always remember to rinse beans under cold running water before adding to a salad.

Feta and Bulgur in Radicchio Cups

The radicchio cups are an attractive way of serving this salad. Alternatively, spoon the bulgur wheat mixture on to a serving plate lined with cos lettuce leaves.

INGREDIENTS

Serves 4

75g/3oz/generous ¾ cup bulgur wheat
60ml/4 tbsp olive oil
juice of 1 lemon, or more to taste
4 spring onions, chopped
90ml/6 tbsp chopped flat leaf parsley
45ml/3 tbsp chopped fresh mint
2 tomatoes, peeled, seeded and diced
175g/6oz/1½ cups feta cheese, cubed
salt and black pepper
1 head radicchio, to serve
flat leaf parsley sprigs, to garnish

1 Place the bulgur wheat in a bowl and soak in cold water for 1 hour. Drain thoroughly in a sieve and press out the excess water.

2 Mix together the oil, lemon juice and seasoning in a bowl. Add the bulgur wheat, then mix well, making sure all the grains are coated with the dressing. Leave at room temperature for about 15 minutes so the bulgur wheat can absorb some of the flavours.

3 Stir in the chopped spring onions, parsley, mint, tomatoes and feta. Taste and adjust the seasoning, adding more lemon juice to sharpen the flavour, if necessary.

4 Separate out the leaves from the radicchio and select the best cup-shaped ones. Spoon a little of the tabbouleh into each one. Arrange on individual plates or on a serving platter and garnish with flat leaf parsley sprigs.

Bresaola, Onion and Rocket Salad

INGREDIENTS

Serves 4

2 onions
75–90ml/5–6 tbsp olive oil
juice of 1 lemon
12 thin slices bresaola
50–75g/2–3oz rocket
salt and black pepper

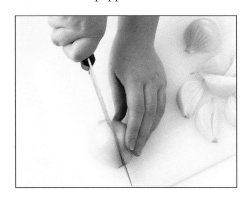

1 Slice each onion into eight wedges through the root.

2 Arrange the onion wedges in a single layer on a grill rack or in a flameproof dish. Brush them with a little of the olive oil and season well with salt and pepper.

3 Place the onion wedges under a hot grill and cook them for about 8–10 minutes, turning once, until they are just beginning to soften and turn golden brown at the edges.

4 Meanwhile, make the dressing: mix together the lemon juice and 60ml/4 tbsp of the olive oil in a small bowl. Add a little salt and black pepper and whisk well until the dressing is thoroughly blended.

5 If you have grilled the onions on a grill rack, then transfer them to a shallow dish once they are cooked.

6 Pour about two-thirds of the dressing over the onion wedges and leave to cool.

7 When the onions are cold, arrange the bresaola slices on individual serving plates with the onions and rocket. Spoon over the remaining dressing and serve at once.

FRUIT SALADS

Fruit is always a fabulous way to end a meal.
In summer, a bowl of red fruits, such as Red Fruit Salad with
strawberries, raspberries and redcurrants, is as near perfection as you
are likely to get. In winter, when soft fruits are unavailable or just
too expensive, try making compotes, such as Autumn Fruit Salad,
with its delicious blend of fruit and fruit juice. Classic fruit salads,
like Orange Salad, are perennial favourites, but for something
more exotic, try Persian Melon Salad, which has an
intriguing and delicate flavour.

Tropical Fruit Salad

This fruit salad can be served for breakfast or as a light dessert.

INGREDIENTS

Serves 4–6

1 pineapple
400g/14oz can guava halves in syrup
2 bananas, sliced
1 large mango, peeled, stoned
  and diced
115g/4oz stem ginger and
  30ml/2 tbsp of the syrup
60ml/4 tbsp thick coconut milk
10ml/2 tsp sugar
2.5ml/½ tsp freshly grated nutmeg
2.5ml/½ tsp ground cinnamon
strips of coconut, to decorate

1 Peel, core and cube the pineapple, and place in a serving bowl. Drain the guavas, reserve the syrup and chop. Add the guavas to the bowl with one of the bananas and the mango.

2 Chop the stem ginger and add it to the pineapple mixture in the bowl.

3 Pour the ginger syrup, and the reserved guava syrup, into a blender or food processor and add the remaining banana, the coconut milk and the sugar. Blend to make a smooth creamy purée.

4 Pour the banana and coconut mixture over the fruit in the serving bowl. Add a little grated nutmeg and a sprinkling of cinnamon. Serve the fruit salad chilled, decorated with strips of coconut.

Avocado Salad in Ginger and Orange Sauce

This is an unusual fruit salad since avocado is more often treated as a vegetable. However, in the Caribbean it is used as a fruit, which of course it is!

INGREDIENTS

Serves 4
2 firm ripe avocados
3 firm ripe bananas, chopped
12 fresh cherries or strawberries
juice of 1 large orange
shredded fresh root ginger (optional)

For the ginger syrup
50g/2oz fresh root ginger, chopped
900ml/1½ pints/3¾ cups water
225g/8oz/1 cup demerara sugar
2 cloves

1 First make the ginger syrup: place the ginger, water, sugar and cloves in a saucepan and bring to the boil. Reduce the heat and simmer for about 1 hour, until well reduced and syrupy.

2 Remove the ginger and discard. Leave to cool. Store in a covered container in the fridge.

3 Peel the avocados, cut into cubes and place in a bowl with the bananas and cherries or strawberries.

4 Pour the orange juice over the fruits. Add 60ml/4 tbsp of the ginger syrup and mix gently, using a metal spoon. Chill the salad in the fridge for about 30 minutes.

5 Add a little shredded ginger, if using, then serve.

Red Fruit Salad

This stunning fruit salad has everything going for it – it can be made in advance; you can make larger quantities of it for parties; it looks superb, and it tastes delicious.

INGREDIENTS

Serves 8
225g/8oz/1 cup raspberries or
    blackberries
50g/2oz/¼ cup redcurrants or
    blackcurrants
30–60ml/2–4 tbsp sugar
8 ripe plums
8 ripe apricots
225g/8oz/1 cup seedless grapes
115g/4oz/½ cup strawberries

1 Mix the berries and currants with 30ml/2 tbsp sugar. Stone the plums and apricots, cut them into pieces and put half of them into a pan with all of the berries.

2 Cook over a very low heat with about 45ml/3 tbsp water, or in a bowl with no water in the microwave, until the fruit is just beginning to soften and the juices are starting to run.

3 Leave to cool slightly and then add the reserved plums and apricots, and the grapes. Taste for sweetness and add more sugar if the fruit is too tart. Leave the fruit salad to cool, cover and chill – overnight if necessary.

4 Just before serving, transfer the fruit to a serving bowl. Slice the strawberries and arrange them over the fruit in the bowl.

COOK'S TIP

The juices from lightly-cooked berries make a brilliant red coating, so make this delicious fruit salad the day before you need it. Serve with Greek-style yogurt, fresh cream, crème fraîche or vanilla ice cream.

Melon and Grapefruit Salad

With its clean, refreshing taste and subtle sweetness, this is the perfect fruit salad. It is simple to make but elegant enough to grace any dinner party.

INGREDIENTS

Serves 4

1 small galia or ogen melon
1 small charentais melon
2 pink grapefruit
45ml/3 tbsp orange juice
60ml/4 tbsp red vermouth
seeds from ½ pomegranate
mint sprigs, to decorate

COOK'S TIP

Ugli fruit makes a good substitute for grapefruit. It is a hybrid of the orange, tangerine and grapefruit, with a yellowy-green skin. The skin is looser and easier to peel than that of a grapefruit and the flesh is deliciously sweet and juicy.

1 Halve the melons lengthwise and scoop out all the seeds. Cut into wedges and remove the skins, then cut across into large bite-size pieces.

2 Using a small sharp knife, cut the peel and pith from the grapefruit. Holding the fruit over a bowl to catch the juice, cut between the grapefruit membranes to release the segments. Set aside the grapefruit segments.

3 Stir the orange juice and vermouth into the bowl containing the reserved grapefruit juice.

4 Arrange the melon pieces and grapefruit segments haphazardly on four individual serving dishes. Spoon the mixed juices over the fruit, then scatter the fruit with the pomegranate seeds. Decorate with mint sprigs and serve at once.

Persian Melon Salad

This is a typical Persian dessert, using a mixture of sweet fresh fruits flavoured with rose-water and aromatic mint.

INGREDIENTS

Serves 4

2 small melons
225g/8oz/1 cup strawberries, plus 4
  to decorate
3 peaches, peeled and cut into
  small cubes
1 bunch seedless grapes (green or red)
30ml/2 tbsp caster sugar
15ml/1 tbsp rose-water
15ml/1 tbsp lemon juice
crushed ice
4 sprigs of mint, to decorate

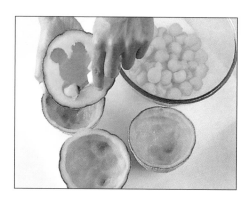

1 Carefully cut the melons in half and remove the seeds. Scoop out the flesh with a melon baller, making sure not to damage the skin. Reserve the melon shells. Alternatively, if you don't have a melon baller, scoop out the flesh using a large spoon and cut into bite-size pieces.

2 Reserve four strawberries and slice the others. Place in a bowl with the melon balls, the peaches, grapes, sugar, rose-water and lemon juice.

3 Pile the fruit into the melon shells and chill in the fridge for 2 hours.

4 To serve, sprinkle with crushed ice, decorating each melon with a whole strawberry and a sprig of mint.

COOK'S TIP

To peel fresh peaches, cover them with boiling water and leave to stand for a couple of minutes. Cool them under cold water before peeling.

Orange Salad

This classic fruit salad is a deserved favourite. The orange flower water adds a wonderfully subtle, delicate taste.

INGREDIENTS

Serves 4
4 oranges
600ml/1 pint/2½ cups water
350g/12oz/1½ cups sugar
30ml/2 tbsp lemon juice
30ml/2 tbsp orange flower water or
   rose-water
50g/2oz/½ cup pistachio nuts, shelled
   and chopped, to decorate

1 Remove the orange part of the rind with a potato peeler.

2 Cut the orange peel into fine strips and boil in several changes of water to remove the bitterness. Drain and set aside until required.

3 Place the water, sugar and lemon juice in a saucepan. Bring to the boil, then add the orange peel and simmer until the syrup thickens. Add the orange flower or rose-water, stir and leave to cool.

4 Completely peel the pith from the oranges and cut them into thick slices. Arrange in a shallow serving dish and pour over the syrup. Chill for about 1–2 hours and then decorate with pistachio nuts and serve.

Emerald Fruit Salad

The cool, green coloured fruits make a refreshing mixture in this delicious fruit salad.

INGREDIENTS

Serves 4
30ml/2 tbsp lime juice
30ml/2 tbsp clear honey
2 green eating apples, cored and sliced
1 small ripe melon, diced
2 kiwi fruit, sliced
1 star fruit, sliced
mint sprigs, to decorate
yogurt or fromage frais, to serve

1 Mix together the lime juice and honey in a large bowl, then toss the apple slices in this.

2 Stir in the melon, kiwi fruit and star fruit. Place in a glass serving dish and chill.

3 Decorate the fruit salad with mint sprigs and serve with yogurt or fromage frais.

--- VARIATION ---

Add other green fruits when available, such as greengages, grapes, pears or kiwano, which is a type of melon. It has a tough yellowy orange rind covered with sharp spikes, and the flesh inside looks like a bright green jelly, encasing edible seeds which can be removed with a spoon.

Autumn Fruit Salad

Despite the name, you can make a version of this fruit salad all year round – just change the fruit to suit the season.

INGREDIENTS

Serves 4

25g/1oz/2 tbsp caster sugar, plus extra
  to taste
juice of 1 lemon
1 red eating apple, cored and sliced
1 green eating apple, cored and sliced
1 eating pear, peeled, cored and sliced
150ml/¼ pint/¾ cup apple or
  pear juice
4 plums or 6–8 sweet damsons, stoned
  and halved or quartered
115g/4oz fresh raspberries,
  blackberries, blueberries or
  strawberries

1 Dissolve the sugar in the lemon juice in a large bowl. As you prepare the apples and pear, put them straight into the lemony syrup.

2 Pour over the apple juice, cover the bowl tightly and leave in a dark place for 2–6 hours.

3 A little while before serving, stir in the rest of the fruit and some more sugar to taste.

Melon and Strawberry Salad

A beautiful and colourful fruit salad, this is suitable to serve as a refreshing appetizer or to round off a meal.

INGREDIENTS

Serves 4

1 galia melon
1 honeydew melon
½ watermelon
225g/8oz/1 cup fresh strawberries
15ml/1 tbsp lemon juice
15ml/1 tbsp clear honey
15ml/1 tbsp chopped fresh mint
1 mint sprig (optional), to garnish

1 Prepare the melons by cutting them in half and discarding the seeds. Use a melon baller to scoop out the flesh into balls, or cut it into cubes with a knife. Place the melon balls (or cubes) in a fruit bowl.

2 Rinse and take the stems off the strawberries, cut these in half and add them to the fruit bowl.

3 Mix together the lemon juice and clear honey with about 15ml/ 1 tbsp of water. Stir carefully to blend and then pour over the fruit. Stir the fruit so that it is thoroughly coated in the lemon and honey mixture.

4 Sprinkle the chopped mint over the top of the fruit. Serve garnished with the mint sprig, if wished.

― COOK'S TIP ―

Use whichever melons are available: substitute cantaloupe for galia or charentais for watermelon, for example. However, try to find three different kinds of melon so that you get variation in colour, and also a variety of textures and flavours.

Fruit Compote

Some of the best fruit salads are a mixture of fresh and dried fruits. This salad features some of the most delicious summer and winter fruits available, but you could experiment with almost any fruit – they combine together beautifully.

INGREDIENTS

Serves 4
115g/4oz dried apricots
115g/4oz dried peaches
115g/4oz prunes
2 oranges, peeled and sliced

For the syrup
1 lemon
4 green cardamom pods
1 cinnamon stick
150ml/¼ pint/¾ cup clear honey
30ml/2 tbsp ginger syrup from the jar
3 pieces stem ginger

1 Soak the apricots, peaches and prunes in enough cold water to cover, for 1–2 hours until they have plumped up.

2 Meanwhile, make the syrup: pare two strips of rind from the lemon with a potato peeler or sharp knife. Halve the lemon and squeeze the juice from one half.

3 Lightly crush the cardamom pods with the back of a large, heavy-bladed knife.

4 Place the lemon rind, cardamom, cinnamon stick, honey, ginger syrup and lemon juice in a heavy-based saucepan. Add 60ml/4 tbsp water, bring to the boil and simmer for 2 minutes. Set aside while making the fruit compote.

5 Drain the apricots, peaches and prunes and cut in half, or quarters if large. Place in a large pan with the oranges. Add 475ml/16fl oz/2 cups water, bring to the boil and simmer for 10 minutes until the fruit is tender.

6 Add the honey and ginger syrup, stir well and simmer for a further 1–2 minutes. Allow the compote to cool, then chill it in the fridge for about 1–2 hours or overnight.

7 Chop the pieces of stem ginger and sprinkle them over the compote just before serving.

Mandarin and Orange Flower Salad

Mandarins, tangerines, clementines, mineolas: any of these lovely citrus fruits are suitable for this recipe.

INGREDIENTS

Serves 4

10 mandarins
15ml/1 tbsp icing sugar
10ml/2 tsp orange flower water
15ml/1 tbsp chopped pistachio nuts

1 Thinly pare a little of the rind from one mandarin and cut it into fine shreds for decoration. Squeeze the juice from two mandarins and reserve it.

2 Peel the remaining fruit, removing as much of the white pith as possible. Arrange the whole fruit in a wide dish.

3 Mix together the reserved mandarin juice, icing sugar and orange flower water, then pour it over the fruit. Cover the dish and chill for at least 1 hour.

4 Blanch the shreds of mandarin rind in boiling water for 30 seconds. Drain, then leave to cool before sprinkling them over the mandarins, with the pistachio nuts.

Minted Melon Salad

Here's a wonderful way to finish a meal. The melon is soaked in a luscious cocktail of fruit juices and tequila, but if you prefer you can make a non-alcoholic version by using extra fruit juice instead of tequila.

INGREDIENTS

Serves 4

2 different melons, such as charentais, cantaloupe, galia, ogen or honeydew

For the cocktail syrup
150ml/¼ pint/¾ cup orange juice
150ml/¼ pint/¾ cup pineapple juice
120ml/4fl oz/½ cup tequila
15ml/1 tbsp chopped fresh mint
15ml/1 tbsp icing sugar
mint sprigs, to decorate

VARIATION

Instead of tequila, use 60ml/4 tbsp orange-flavoured liqueur, such as Cointreau or Grand Marnier. Add 15ml/1 tbsp honey to replace the icing sugar.

1 Halve the melons and scoop out the seeds using a metal spoon. Cut the melons into thin wedges using a sharp knife and remove the skins.

2 Arrange the two different varieties of melon wedges alternately on four individual serving plates.

3 Whisk the orange juice, pineapple juice, tequila, mint and sugar in a bowl, until the sugar has dissolved.

4 Pour the syrup over the melon and decorate with mint sprigs. Chill for about 30 minutes before serving.

Index